DESTINATION: CHEF

A Culinary Training Program Guide to Becoming Food Service-Ready in Ten Weeks

Chef Timothy Tucker &

Amanda Eaton

Cover photos and design by Amanda Eaton.

Kroc Center illustrations and photos by Michael Guadarrama.

ISBN: 1537771523

First Printing: October 2016

CONTENTS

This book is dedicated to all the students—past, present, and future-- to pass through the Culinary Arts Training Programs that necessitated the writing of this book.

The authors would like to thank Launa Schweitzer for her help with the preparation of this manuscript.

DESTINATION: CHEF

A Culinary Training Program Guide to Becoming Food Service-Ready in Ten Weeks

Introduction

"No one who cooks, cooks alone. Even at her most solitary, a cook in the kitchen is surrounded by generations of cooks past, the advice and menus of cooks present, the wisdom of cookbook writers."

--Laurie Colwin

This book was created to be the primary textbook for a ten-week accelerated Culinary Arts Training Program. The course, the brainchild of Chef Timothy Tucker, is designed to teach students from all walks of life the basics of cooking in a professional kitchen.

In addition to classroom time and traditional lectures, the program incorporates many hours spent in a teaching kitchen (after completion, students will have spent more classtime actually cooking than most two-year culinary students), as well as preparation for the ServSafe Manager's Certification test given at approximately the nine-week mark*.

Each class—or "semester," culminates in a graduation ceremony featuring dishes chosen, planned, and cooked by the students. They are encouraged to showcase their skills and talents at this gathering of family, friends, local sponsors, and government officials (past classes have cooked

* Note that this book was designed to be used together with the most recent ServSafe guide.

for Massachusetts governor Charlie Baker, Boston Police Commissioner William Evans, and many more!).

Through dozens of classes in several states, the programs' students have gone on to become line cooks, restaurant chefs, food truck workers, and even restaurant and small business owners.

After completion of the course, the CATP staff work to refer students to gainful employment in the field, as well as provide support as they pursue their career and life goals.

The overall result? A coterie of graduates who have the knowledge, skills, and connections to begin a fulfilling career in the culinary industry.

Goals for students in each class include the following:

* Learn and master the fundamentals of cooking a variety of meals in different styles and from different cultures. Abilities should meet or exceed the requirements for cooking in a professional kitchen, including knife skills, recipe interpretation and creation abilities, and the development of a discerning palette.

* Learn about food culture: what good food is, where it comes from, and how to cook in a sustainable, environmentally- responsible, and healthy manner.

* Develop and master the necessary "soft" skills needed to become employed and thrive in a workplace. This includes successful conflict resolution, time management, self-motivation skills, and interviewing abilities, as well as completion of a professional resume.

* Use the knowledge and experience gained to improve the circumstances of the student's own life, as well as the lives of their family members and community.

STARTING ON YOUR JOURNEY

At the very beginning of the course, students should contemplate the following questions:

- *Who am I-- as a cook, a worker, and a person?*
- *Why am I here? What goals do I want to achieve?*
- *How can I expect the course to help me reach my goals? What things will I need to do personally to succeed?*
- *What experience, knowledge, and talents do I bring to the classroom? To the workplace?*
- *Where do I want to be in my life and career at the end of this course? One year from now? Five years from now?*

In order to provide direction to the last question, all students take the following short quiz, which appears in several cooking sources, including a New York Times blog[i]. (Answers have been slightly altered for our purposes.)

What's Your Cooking Personality?

1.) When I prepare a meal, I typically:

a.) Rely on classic dishes my family has always enjoyed
b.) Substitute more healthful ingredients
c.) Follow the recipe step-by-step
d.) Rarely use recipes and like to experiment
e.) Go out all to impress my guests

2.) Some of my favorite ingredients are:

a.) Lots of bread, starches, and red meat
b.) Fish and vegetables

c.) Beef and chicken
d.) Vegetables, spices, and unusual ingredients
e.) A trendy ingredient I saw on TV

3.) In my free time, I like to:
a.) Visit with friends and family
b.) Exercise or take a fitness class
c.) Organize the house
d.) Take part in creative or artistic pursuits
e.) Be spontaneous and seek adventure

4.) My favorite things to cook are:
a.) Home-baked goodies
b.) Foods with fresh ingredients and herbs
c.) Casseroles
d.) Ethnic foods and wok dishes
e.) Anything that lets me fire up the grill

5.) Other people describe me as:
a.) Really friendly
b.) Health-conscious
c.) Diligent and methodical
d.) Curious
e.) Intense

Mostly a's: Giving Cook

22% of all cooks out there are part of this category! They are concerned with tradition and spend time perfecting their family's favorite dishes. Family recipes going back several generations and comfort foods are important to this type.

If you are a Giving cook, you might want to consider a career as a personal chef/ home cook, where you can consider the needs and wants of specific individuals that you know well, or at a school or camp. A career as a baker

or pastry chef also suits this nurturing personality type.

Mostly b's: Health-Conscious Cook

The Health-Conscious cook is concerned with the wholesomeness of food over all other qualities. Fish and fresh herbs, veggies, and fruits provide opportunities to experiment and still feel good about what they are serving. This category contains about 20% of all cooks.

If you are a Health-Conscious cook, you might want to consider a career working in a health food restaurant, garden, or farm where fresh ingredients originate. Nursing homes and hospitals, where health is always a consideration when preparing dishes, are also good options.

Mostly c's: Innovative Cook

The Innovative Cook is concerned with trends and creativity. Eschewing traditional recipes, they favor experimentation and are more concerned with trying new cooking styles and ingredients, yet still turning out something delicious! About 19% of all cooks fall into this category.

On-trend restaurants that boast a global menu appeal to Innovative cooks, as does a career in food photography (to utilize your creative side) or a career as a Research & Development Chef.

Mostly d's: Methodical Cook

Methodical cooks are concerned with following recipes to the letter and want to get the exact same resulting dish every time they make it. Plating and arranging the food just so and making sure a steak is exactly the right color are super important to these folks. 18% of cooks are Methodical Cooks.

Careers you should consider as a Methodical are line cook in a high quality restaurant or an upscale hotel where the consistency and look of

d is just as important as the taste. Catering could also appeal, as ... as a career as a TV cook, where you can show everyone the exact methods you use to prepare your famous dishes!

Mostly e's: Competitive Cook

Competitive cooks represent only 13% of all cooks, but they want everyone to know they are #1! They thrive on competition with other chefs and professionals and seek out positions that will give them enviable status. Compliments are music to their ears!

High-end gourmet restaurants with great reputations and lots of opportunity for advancement is where Competitive cooks will be happiest. The more you can enter your food into competitions like Chili Cookoffs to gain prestige, the better! And you love interacting with diners, who will no doubt be very impressed with your output.

SKILLS AND GOALS

Now that you have some idea where you are going and why you are here, you will need to know what specific skills and techniques you should be able to demonstrate after completion of the course. The items on the list below are some of the things that your instructor and eventually, employer, will be looking for in a graduate.

Food Safety

- ☐ Demonstrate thorough and correct handwashing procedures.
- ☐ Demonstrate steps to avoid contamination and cross-contamination of food.
- ☐ Is able to store, cook, and hold different types of food correctly.
- ☐ Is able to clean and sanitize foodservice equipment correctly.

Workplace Safety

- ☐ Demonstrates and follows safety procedures designed to prevent burns and scalds to self and others.
- ☐ Demonstrates and follows safety procedures designed to prevent slips and falls.
- ☐ Recognizes, holds, uses, and passes knives correctly.

Kitchen Knowledge

- ☐ Is able to read, comprehend, and follow instructions, recipes, menus, and policies.
- ☐ Weighs and measures food/ ingredients accurately and properly.
- ☐ Converts weights and measurements as appropriate.
- ☐ Stocks and replenishes food, beverages, condiments, and sundries at all appropriate stations.
- ☐ Uses, handles, and cleans all cooking, washing, and waste disposal equipment correctly.
- ☐ Is able to receive all food and beverages. Examines product for defects.
- ☐ Is able to create, maintain, and adjust an inventory. Regularly audits inventory to assure sanitation and safety.
- ☐ Accurately labels all food and ingredients in storage.

Food Knowledge

- ☐ Is able to recognize, prepare, and store all foods and ingredients correctly.
- ☐ Provides and/or calculates nutritional information for dishes and ingredients.

Industry Knowledge

- ☐ Is able to cost out dishes and prepare appropriate menus.
- ☐ Is able to plate, garnish, and present all dishes appropriately.
- ☐ Is able to properly and correctly address customers' questions and concerns.
- ☐ Makes appropriate recommendations to diners.
- ☐ Is knowledgeable about restaurant tipping and payment policies.

General Employment Skills

- ☐ Presents an appropriate resume and work history. Is able to furnish proper references.
- ☐ Speaks and listens carefully, clearly, and with courtesy to clients and colleagues.
- ☐ Asks appropriate questions and seeks supervisory approval as needed.
- ☐ Presents a friendly, enthusiastic and knowledgeable demeanor to customers and co-workers.
- ☐ Demonstrates proper judgement and makes appropriate decisions.
- ☐ Arrives to work on time; follows proper call-out procedures when an absence is necessary.
- ☐ Arrives to work dressed appropriately and properly prepared for the day.
- ☐ Is able to write simple business notes and/or letters.
- ☐ Is able to answer the phone and address inquiries with knowledge and courtesy.

Think about which of these skills you have already mastered, and which ones you will need to work on. (They will all be addressed in this book, with the exception of the safety and sanitation information-- which will be in your ServSafe manual.)

INTRODUCTORY ACTIVITY: THE SUPERTASTER TEST

Within the first few days of class, students often perform the supertasters test. Approximately 25% of the population is made of up of what's called supertasters—people who sense taste with a greater intensity than others. About 50% of the population is made up of normal tasters, and the remaining 25% are non-tasters, or those are who are less sensitive to taste than the average person.

How do we tell what category we fall into? Follow these simple steps[ii]:

1.) Gather a sheet of paper with hole(s) (should be the size created by a standard office hole puncher) in it, a magnifying glass, a friend, and some blue dye/ food coloring.

2.) Dab the blue food coloring on the front third of your tongue (use a mirror if you need guidance). You should notice that this area is densest with papillae, or tiny dots on the tongue that contain taste buds. The coloring should stain your tongue, but not the papillae.
3.) Place the paper on your tongue, so that the hole frames the area where you see the most papillae.
4.) Using the magnifying glass, have your friend count the number of papillae visible within the hole/ circle. Each papillae bump will contain approximately 4 tastebuds!
5.) Use the following chart to see where you stand:

# of Papillae Visible	*Status*
Less than 15	Non-taster
15-30	Normal/ average taster
More than 30	Supertaster

The differences in taster status are usually due to genetics (for instance, women are twice as likely as men to be supertasters. Those with Asian, South American, and African heritage are also more likelyiii. However, this is not to suggest that average or non-tasters cannot be great cooks!).

Note that taste buds can also be damaged due to burns, smoking, alcohol, eating very spicy/ sour foods, etc. This may interfere with your ability to taste, but since taste buds have the ability to heal quickly, any injury is usually temporary.

1. Kitchen Equipment & Terms

"Always start out with a larger pot than what you think you need."

--Julia Child

One of the most important things to remember in culinary arts is the phrase *mis en place*. Quite simply, this translates from the French to "put in place," and describes the concept that everything you will need (e.g. ingredients, knives, utensils) should be prepared, set up, organized, and arranged before you begin to work or your shift begins.

A successful cook in a commercial kitchen will duly prepare for situations both routine (preparing food) and emergency (an unexpected influx of guests, breakdown of a piece of equipment) that could happen in a restaurant.

Let's take a look at the most common kitchen utensils and equipment used in the professional culinary industry. (These will often be different from what you use in a home kitchen.)

Figure 1 / Photo: The Kroc Center

In the photo above, we can see from left to right: spider, offset spatula, ladle, wooden spoon, grater, slotted spoon, whisk, recyclable plastic container, scale.

The *spider* is a tool used to retrieve items from a fryer or skim the tops of liquids like soup.

The *offset spatula* is used to turn, lift, and flip items on a grill.

The *ladle* is used for spooning liquids like soup or stew.

A *wooden spoon* is used to stir soups and sauces; wooden utensils should always be used when working with non-stick or delicate cookware.

A *grater* is used to grate things like cheeses.

The *slotted spoon* is used for anything that liquid should be drained out of, e.g. green beans that are cooked in liquid.

The *whisk* is used to efficiently mix together ingredients; a proper whisking technique is something that cannot be underestimated in a culinary career!

You should always store ingredients in a recyclable *plastic container* as shown in the photo. This way, it is very easy to place a plastic Saran wrap cover over the top to keep contents fresh.

The *kitchen scale* is used to weigh the amount of an ingredient. This can be very important when cooking from a recipe.

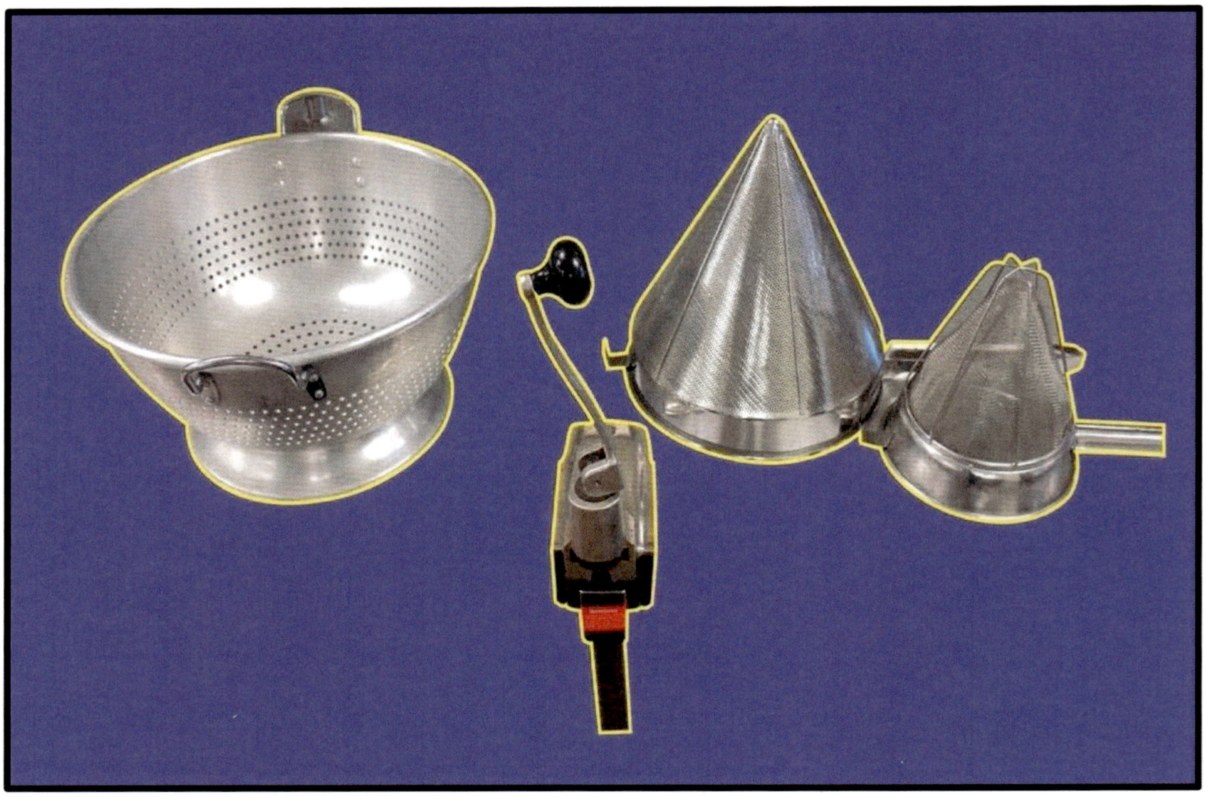

Figure 2/ Photo: The Kroc Center

In Figure 2, you might recognize the item on the far left, a large *colander*, or strainer. However, many students are unfamiliar with the item with the metal handle that is clamped onto the table—this is an *industrial can opener*! Make sure to clean and sanitize the can opener daily. (One of the surest ways to tell that someone is a rookie in a professional kitchen is their inability to operate the can opener, so be sure to learn well!)

The *China cap* and *chinois* (sheen-WAH), to the right of the photo, are both strainers for stocks and sauces (the mesh of the chinois is especially fine).

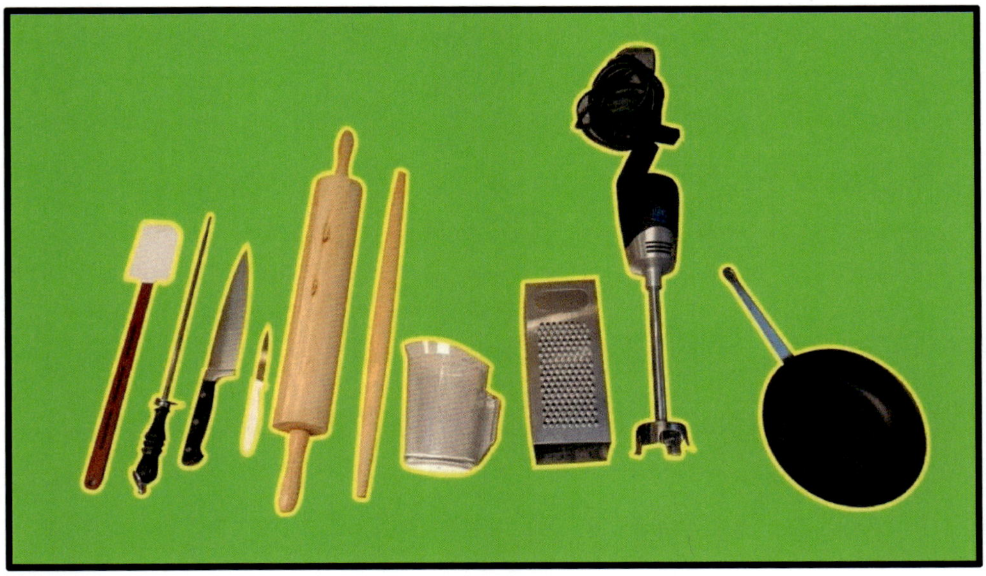

Figure 3/ Photo: The Kroc Center

In Figure 3, we can see from left to right: rubber spatula, steel, chef knife, paring knife, rolling pin, French rolling pin, measuring cup, grater, and a hand mixer.

The *rubber spatula* is used to cook with non-stick or Teflon cookware. It is very important to use only wooden or rubber utensils with this kind of cookware as metal ones can scratch off the carcinogenic coating. We certainly would not want this to get into our cooking!

The *sharpening steel* is used for sharpening and straightening knife blades. Blades should be drawn along the entire length, on each side. Knives should be sharpened after every 3-4 hours of use to keep them from becoming dull.

The *chef knife* is, as its name suggests, one of the best all-around, go-to knives in your kitchen arsenal. Its uses are wide and varied; you will definitely be using this for almost every task (see "Using a Knife" further in this chapter).

The *paring knife* is used for cutting small things like lemons. It can also be used to peel.

A *rolling pin* is used in baking, to flatten and spread out doughs and other breads.

The *French rolling pin* serves the same function as the more common rolling pin to its left. However, it is more compact and simple, being only a single piece (similar to a mini baseball bat).

Measuring cups are, true to their name, used for measuring amounts of ingredients! These can be used for liquid or dry ingredients.

The *hand mixer* is a small version of a stand mixer and blender. However, this can fit into smaller equipment, such as pots, allowing you to bring the tool to the ingredients, rather than the other way around.

Figure 4/ Photo: The Kroc Center

In Figure 4 above, we see: a potato masher, bench scraper/ pastry cutter, food brush, pepper grinder, potato peeler, plastic funnel, and measuring cup.

No matter the cuisine or style, the *potato masher* is important because mashed potatoes are a very popular dish. It can also be used for soups and sauces, when chunks of soft ingredients need to be broken up and stirred into the rest of the liquid.

The *bench scraper/ pastry cutter* (both names are equally popular) is used in baking to cut dough and scrape flour off of the top.

The *food brush* resembles a regular paintbrush and is used to spread butters or marinades over meats and bread.

The *pepper grinder* grinds small balls of pepper.

(The *potato peeler* and *measuring cups* are self-explanatory.)

The *funnel* is used for the pouring of liquids that need to get into a small mouth, such as pouring infused vinegar into a narrow vinegar bottle.

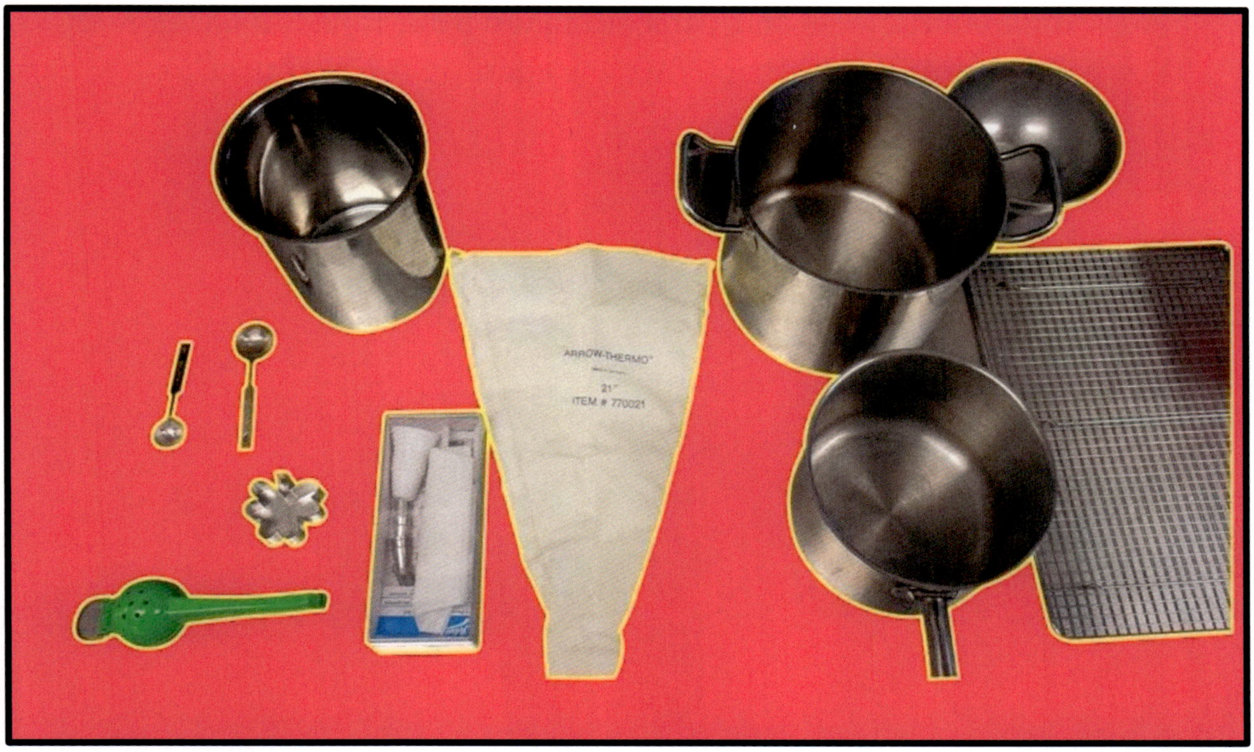

Figure 5/ Photo: The Kroc Center

In Figure 5 above, we can see (from left to right): Teaspoon, tablespoon, cookie cutter, green lime juicer, tips with pastry bag, bain marie, stockpot, saucepan, measuring bowl, rack.

The cone-shaped *pastry bag* can be filled with frosting or whipped cream and attached to different types of *pastry tips* (the piece with the narrow silver tip), which are used to "draw" different types of designs.

When it comes to pots and pans, most are self-explanatory and familiar to those who have worked in a home kitchen before, but let's talk about the different types shown in the photo.

Stockpots are tall, deep pots usually used for making large quantities of liquid-heavy dishes like soups, stews, or rice. They are described in quarts (i.e. a two- or three-quart stockpot).

Saucepans are what most people consider to be "regular pans." They are available in many sizes, can be used to cook almost anything, and are ideal for simmering and boiling. (Smaller, mini versions of saucepans are called *milk pans*.)

The material pots and pans are made from is also important to how they will perform in a kitchen. (See the chart on the next page.)

Materials for Kitchen Pots & Pans

Aluminum: Inexpensive, lightweight but strong, good conductor of heat. Best for sautéing, frying.

Anodized Aluminum: Aluminum that has been treated with a finish to prevent corrosion. Usually non-stick, but vulnerable to scratches.

Cast Iron: Heavy, can be expensive and break easily. Known for its even distribution of heat. Best for deep frying and slow cooking. Usually not found in restaurants.

Copper: Can be expensive, heats and cools down quickly. Good for sautéing, frying. Can leave a metallic aftertaste in food (esp. when cooking salty dishes). Polish regularly.

Glass Usually tempered glass; holds heat well but slow to heat up and can heat unevenly. Good for microwave use, as well as in the stove and oven.

Non-stick: Best for omelettes or reheating foods that are sticky (such as rice or pasta); need less fat when cooking. Vulnerable to scratching, which chips toxic materials into food. Use with wooden utensils only.

Porcelain: Usually enameled; best for oven use.

Stainless Steel: Good strength, versatility, and shiny look, non-corroding. However, one of the least heat-responsive materials. The most commonly used material in restaurants.

Figure 6/ Photo: The Kroc Center

In Figure 6 above, we can see, from left to right: Sterno, coffee press, coffee grinder, coffee carafe, coffee percolator, rice cooker/ steamer, Cambro. The orange item in the back of the picture is a salad spinner.

A *sterno* is something that you light with flame to provide heat. A chafing dish containing the food to be heated would traditionally be placed over it. Sternos are used at many catering events to keep food heated.

Coffee presses, in this case a French press, are used to efficiently prepare coffee. First, fresh whole coffee beans are crushed in a coffee grinder and then placed into the press, along with boiling water. The top part of the press is then used to press down (hence the name) the beans and brew the coffee. The finished coffee is then placed into the carafe for serving.

A *coffee percolator* is another piece of equipment used to brew coffee, usually reserved for more complex or gourmet blends. Water is continuously cycled through the ground beans until the coffee reaches the desired strength.

The *rice cooker/ steamer* is an accessory typically used to cook rice; it can also be used to steam vegetables.

A *Cambro* (referred to by its most common brand name, much like a Keurig coffeemaker) is an insulated box used to transport hot foods to other locations, keeping contents at 140°F.

The *salad spinner* is a kitchen tool designed to remove extra water from salad greens. This is very important as no one wants to serve (or eat!) a damp or limp salad. Putting greens through a salad spinner also allows dressing to better stick to salad ingredients.

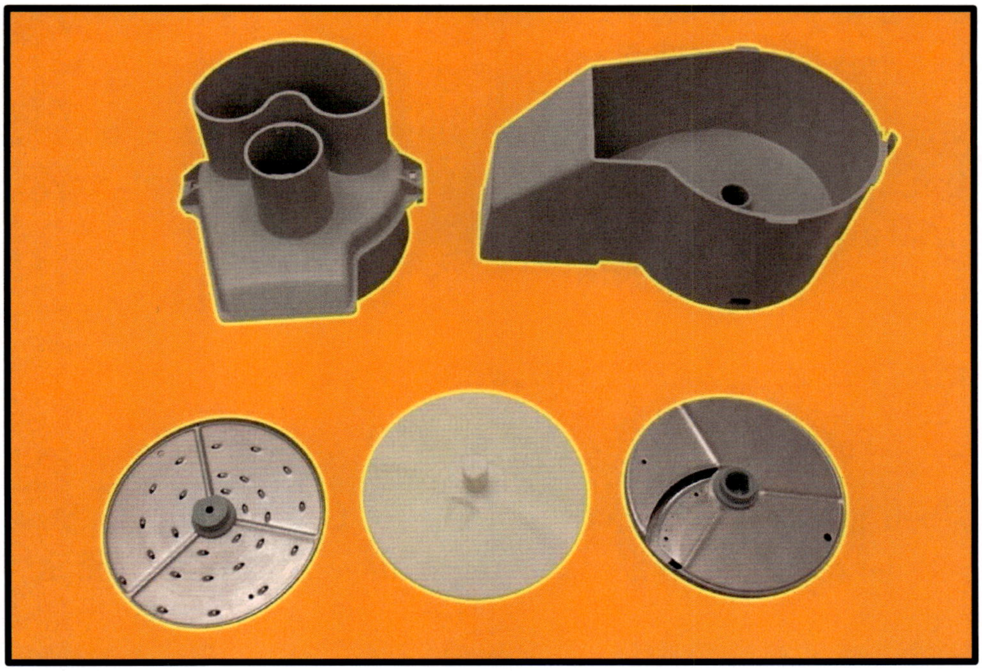

Figure 7/ Photo: The Kroc Center

In Figure 7 above, we can see the different attachments for the *food processor*, which is used to chop or puree food. The food processor can be one of the most difficult pieces of equipment for students to learn in the kitchen-- not because it is difficult to use, but because it is so hard to assemble correctly. All the pins must align perfectly for it to operate, so this make take some practice! You will need to select the grater or slicer piece.

Keeping in the classic kitchen tradition of *mis en place*, it is very important to keep your utensils organized and easy to find. I suggest labeling all drawers and storage areas so that no one is confused about where items should be returned to.

Remember to assign appropriate places for your items. For instance, knives should be stored in a place where their blades will not touch or rub against other knife blades or equipment. (Special knife holders or paper/ cardboard sleeves can also be used.) Sanitized utensils or equipment should not be stored with unsantized tools.

Do not give into the laziness or stress of the moment and just throw your utensils anywhere, no matter how tired or busy you are! This will just cause problems later down the road.

Now that you are familiar with the basics used in a kitchen, we are ready to move onto the larger pieces of equipment that you might see in a commercial kitchen.

COMMERCIAL KITCHEN EQUIPMENT

When it comes to commercial kitchen equipment, it is both similar and dissimilar to the equipment you might have in a home kitchen. Though many utensils such as spoons and whisks will be the same, students often need to relearn the can opener, the food processor, and the slicer and mixer for the industrial kitchen. Keep in mind that unlike in your home, the commercial kitchen is built for volume—feeding a mass of diners as efficiently as possible!

First, let's examine the types of pans that are typically used in food service. Looking at Figure 8, we see a *chafing dish*. Resembling a deep pan, the chafing dish is raised up above a heat source such as a sterno to keep food warm and/or covered away from the kitchen; they are commonly used at buffets and other large meals. Though the chafing dish pictured is rectangular (the most popular type found in food service), chafing dishes can also be round or square and have a variety of different lids and tops.

Figure 8/ Photo: Timothy Tucker

Figure 9/ Photo: Timothy Tucker

In Figure 9, we can see a variety of *hotel pans.* Hotel pans are sized to industry standards and designed to fit into chafing dishes to hold food. You could place an entire pan into the dish (as the pan on the left is sized for), or place several simultaneously, as in the pans on the right. Metal pans are used for hot foods, whereas hotel pans for cold foods are usually made of plastic (in the Figure 9 photo, one hotel pan is made of plastic).

Accordingly, hotel pans are described based on their fit into a chafing dish, i.e. half pans, where two pans can fit into a single chafing dish; fourth pans, where four can fit; eigth pans, where eight can fit, and so on.

They are also described based on the depth of the pan. Hotel pans come in depths of 2 inches, 4 inches, and 6 inches. Therefore, a "4-inch half pan" would refer to a hotel pan that is *a.)* 4 inches in depth, and *b.)* of the size where two pans would fit into the chafing dish.

Sometimes to adequately fit all the pans into the chafing dish, a tool called an *adapter* is needed. An adapter resembles a rail; it is placed parallel to the edge of the chafing dish to hold the pans up where a real edge might not be available. The adapter holds the pans steadily in place.

The large *floor-model mixer*, pictured in Figure 10, is an important tool in the professional kitchen. This machine is built especially for mixing and processing large quantities of food. Just like smaller mixers, it uses beaters, driven by gears, to blend ingredients together.

Figure 10/ Photo: The Kroc Center

Combi ovens, like the one pictured in Figure 10, are ovens that can operate as either convection (dry) or steam (wet) ovens, or both simultaneously. They are self-cleaning, versatile machines and are useful for many cooking methods. They are also able to store hot food, functioning as a holding cabinet. Most have a probe inside that measures food temperature, allowing you to cook the food to the specification desired.

Keep in mind that because of the speed and efficiency of a convection oven, you should always cook 25°- 50°F *lower* in a convection oven than when using a standard oven. Check temperatures of food carefully with the probes, as cooking times might also be shorter.

In a well-equipped professional kitchen, you will often see a *gas burner*, as shown in Figure 11. Gas burners can heat food very quickly and are the burners of choice for commercial food preparation.

In Figure 12 on page 31, we can also see the *flat-top grill*. The "flat-top" refers to the steel plate that covers the burners. When the burners beneath are on, pots that may be too heavy or large for the burners themselves can be heated by placing them on the steel surface. This appliance creates a very hot and even surface for cooking, and somewhat resembles a griddle.

Figure 10/ Photo: The Kroc Center

Figure 11/ Photo: The Kroc Center

Figure 12/ Photo: The Kroc Center

A *grill* with a splatter guard on three sides is shown in Figure 13 (second appliance from left). This will be very similar to the outdoor grills that many people use to barbeque in the summer. The splatter guard protects surrounding equipment from dabs of hot oil or grease.

The *deep fryer*, shown in Figure 14, will be familiar to those of you who have worked in the fast food industry. It uses hot fat to cook food such as French fries and potato chips. The baskets are used to lift the food out of the oil once it has completed cooking.

Figure 13/ Photo: The Kroc Center

Figure 14/ Photo: The Kroc Center

USING A KNIFE

One of the important skills to master in the kitchen is becoming quick and proficient with a knife. Knife skills will be called upon constantly in a kitchen, for virtually every dish you will make.

First of all, let's take a look at the different kinds of knives usually found in a kitchen (see Figure 16 on the next page). In this knife kit, we can see (from left to right): the *paring knife*, *boning knife*, *serrated knife*, *chef knife*, and *sharpening steel*. These are the essential knives that every culinary professional should know. Each knife in your arsenal will have different specialties and uses. (See the chart on the page 36 for a handy explanation!)

Note that each knife will have a *cutting edge*, or edge of the blade; a *tip*, the thin, narrow top of the blade; and the *heel*, the thick part of the knife that caps the *grip,* or section where the knife is grasped by the hand. (See the knife diagram below.)

Knife Diagram/ Photo: Timothy Tucker

Figure 15/ Photo: Timothy Tucker

Types of Knives and Their Uses

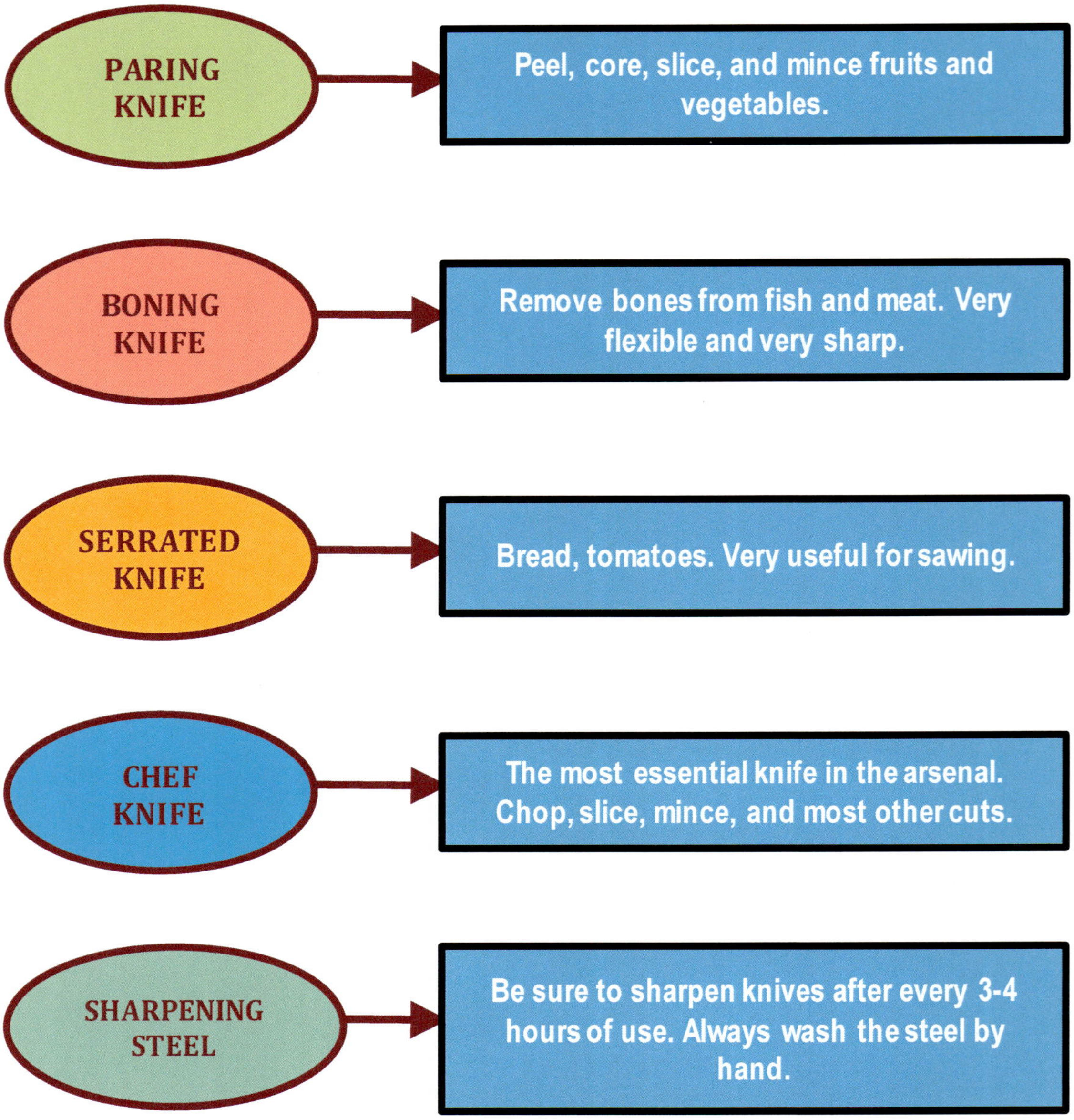

Many students are afraid that becoming expert at using knives means suffering many cuts along the way. Though every chef has cut him/ herself at least a few times, most cuts can be avoided by simply paying attention and keeping your hand in a C-clamp position, as in Figure 16. (You will need to adjust this basic hand position according to the type of knife you are using, as in Figure 17.)

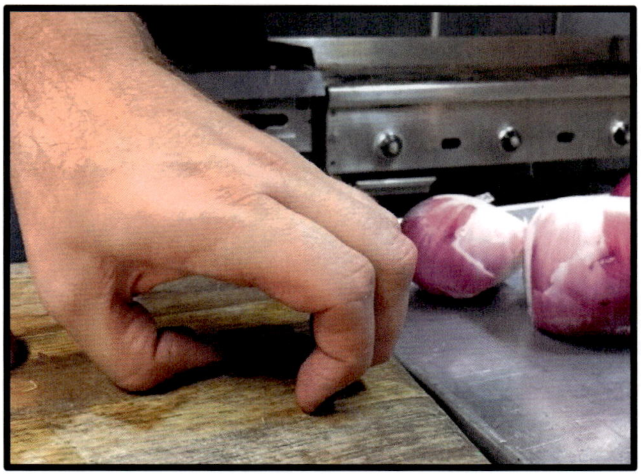

Figure 16/ Photo: Timothy Tucker

Figure 17/ Photo: Timothy Tucker

Your grip on the knife should be strong enough to control it, but not so tight that your hand will get tired with repetitious use. Use one hand to manage the knife with smooth, even, controlled strokes away from yourself, a technique called rocking the knife, where the knife's cutting edge does not leave the cutting surface. Use the other to hold the food that is being cut.

Of course, it bears repeating that the safest knife is a sharp knife! Dull knives require more pressure to cut properly, and therefore add chances for injury. Make sure to sharpen your knives regularly (every 3-4 hours).

There are several kinds of cuts that will be necessary to know to work in any professional kitchen (see Figure 19; not to scale). The definitions are in the chart below. Work at becoming familiar with each of these cuts.

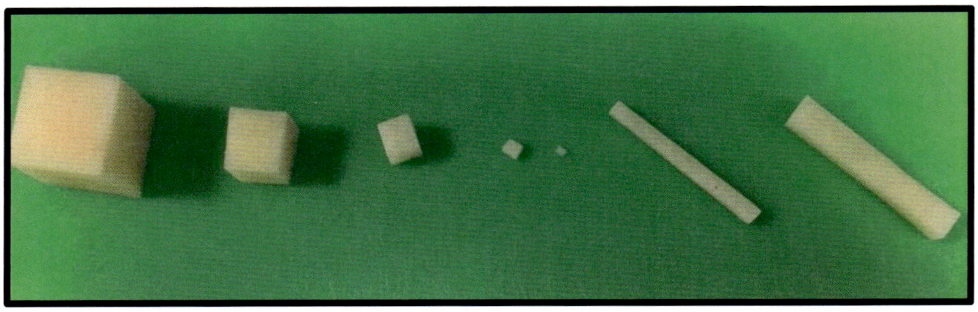

Figure 18/ Photo: Timothy Tucker

Name	Shape	Dimensions
Large dice	Cube	3/4" x 3/4" x 3/4"
Medium dice	Cube	1/2" x 1/2" x 1/2"
Small dice	Cube	1/4" x 1/4" x 1/4"
Brunoise	Cube	1/8" x 1/8" x 1/8"
Fine brunoise	Cube	1/16" x 1/16" x 1/16"
Julienne	Stick	1/8" x 1/8" x 2"
Batonnet	Stick	1/4" x 1/4" x 2"

As you may have noticed, *dicing* is a procedure used when cutting something into a cube shape. Usually, this involves first cutting the item into a stick shape using the julienne or batonnet cuts.

COOKING METHODS & BEST PRACTICES

Though there are numerous cooking methods, you will only need to know the most commonly used ones (described in the chart on page 40) to begin your culinary career right away. Read the chart carefully, as some are "dry" cooking methods, and some refer to "wet" ingredients. A few are even a combination of the two.

As far as best practices go, we all know that working in a production line can be hectic. The pressure of having many tasks to perform before a dish can be finished can be stressful for the cook.

Generally, it is preferable to complete one task before beginning another; for example, say a dish calls for half-mooned squash. It is far more efficient to wash all the squash in one go, then cut them all in one go, than to wash one and cut it, then move onto the second one. This way, one motion of a task is finished before moving on to the next one, much like on an assembly line.

It is also helpful to take a few moments every so often throughout the day to make sure your station, stovetop, and sink (if applicable) are clean--not only for sanitary purposes, but to allow you to perform tasks more efficiently.

Though kitchen towels and/or rags are an essential part of a functioning kitchen, try not to use more than two towels per day (as sanitation and conditions allow). Laundry service fees for kitchen towels can really add up if staff is careless with their linen use!

Always be thinking of the shift or employee who is coming after you. If you are working a closing shift, make sure your area is as clean as possible for staff that will be coming in to work the next day. If someone will be taking over your shift, confirm that everything has been set up properly for their arrival, so that they can get to work smoothly without disrupting the flow of back-of-the-house operations. This will also ensure more harmonius relationships with your colleagues.

Though it seems counterintuitive to the stressful, fast-moving existence of a cook in a bustling restaurant, try to practice calm and deliberateness. You will accomplish more correctly if you take time to successfully orient yourself. What task are you performing? What is the most efficient way to do it? What steps and tools will you need? Seek guidance from your superiors if you are having difficulties performing a task. (It is better to ask questions than to be berated for screwing up the food!)

And lastly, take care to reign in your personal demons. Due to the long hours and stress of their positions, restaurant workers have traditionally been prone to alcoholism and drug addiction. Though being friendly and socializing with your co-workers is positive and beneficial, it will only hurt your career to give in to peer pressure to overindulge in drugs or alcohol.

You cannot grow to become a great chef, or even a respected colleague at work, if you come in too hung over or drugged out to remember your basic job duties. You want to look at every job as a stepping stone on the path to your dream career—don't let one or two nights of careless behavior spoil it!

Cooking Methods				
		Wet	**Dry**	**Comb.**
Bake	*Cooking done in an oven using dry heat.*		✓	
Boil	*Bringing a liquid to its boiling point (212°F on a stove, 210°F on a stove with salt).*	✓		
Braise	*Meat and/ or vegetables are browned in fat, then cooked within a tightly covered container, with a small amount of liquid, over a long period of time. Also known as the "low and slow" method of cooking.*			✓
Broil	*To cook directly above or below a heat source. Food is broiled in an oven.*		✓	
Deep Fry	*Cooking using hot fryer oil. The food is usually totally submerged in the oil while cooking.*		✓	
Grill	*Cooking on high heat, usually on a grill. When grilling meats, wait until the meat "releases " (pulls easily off the grill) before removing it from the heat. Obvious grill markings should be visible.*		✓	
Pan Fry	*Similar to deep frying, but the food is only partially submerged in oil.*		✓	
Poach	*Cooked gently in liquid at a temperature just below the boiling point (160°F-180°F).*	✓		
Roast	*Cooking in an oven utilizing heat higher than in baking. This method requires fat and takes place within an uncovered container.*		✓	
Sauté	*To cook with low fat and high heat.*		✓	
Simmer	*Cooking that takes place between 185°F-200°F, usually after the product has been brought to a boil. Cooks will often bring the temperature down to a simmer because boiling is very harsh on flavors. To avoid "cooking out" flavors, the food should be allowed to continue heating at this lower temperature range.*	✓		
Steam	*Much like boiling, this method uses the 212° boiling point of liquids, but uses the moisture from boiling to heat the food rather than heat alone.*	✓		
Stew	*Food is simmered slowly over a long period of time in a covered container. Ingredients are only barely covered with liquid. This method tenderizes meat and gives flavors time to fully "marry," or combine.*			✓

BASIC KITCHEN DUTIES

Every culinary professional should have a good handle on the basic kitchen tasks that need to be peformed, both when opening and closing the kitchen for the day. Take a look at some of these below:

Opening Duties-- Make sure to:

□ Consult with kitchen leadership to determine the "game plan" for the day. Take a look at the day's menu as well to know what to expect.

□ Check the walk-in freezer and other food storage areas to ensure that food and ingredients are properly stored and labeled, and that all needed product is fresh and available for the beginning of the day. Pull and organize what is needed for your station, including any fresh ice.

□ Put out those ingredients that need to thaw or marinate.

□ Fully stock your station, including condiments and appropriate cleaning/ sanitation supplies, such as gloves and hairnets.

□ Ensure good working order of equipment (burners, lamps, pans, utensils, etc.).

□ Ensure that the line of sight, or any areas that are visible from the dining or public area, are presentable and clean.

Closing Duties-- Make sure that:

□ All food is properly labeled and stored. Check freezer and other food storage areas to make sure they are swept, uncluttered, and clean.

□ Soiled towels and linens have been put in the correct place for cleaning.

□ All areas, including grill tops, sneeze guards, counters, etc. have been cleaned and/or wiped down. This includes any draining of fryers, etc.

Check the sinks and other equipment for cleanliness.

☐ Before leaving, make sure all equipment has been turned off! Many a kitchen worker has been woken up in the middle of the night due to fears about leaving something on in the kitchen!

2. Food Basics

"If it came from a plant, eat it. If it was made in a plant, don't."

--Michael Pollan

For something so essential to sustain life, food can be a complex topic, especially for the culinary professional. Food is quite literally their "bread and butter," another phrase that speaks to the importance of eating in our society!

Though people who choose a culinary career are most likely very familiar with food, it never hurts to go over the basics.

MEASUREMENTS

Some of the most important food basics to cover are units of measurement. These are used to standardize, describe, and portion out quantities of food and ingredients, both wet and dry.

The most common units of measurement vary according to location; the metric system is most common globally. However, volume-based units are standard for the United States. (See the chart on page 44.)

MEASUREMENT EQUIVALENTS

1	Gallon	=	4	Quarts	1	Quart	=	2	Pints
		=	8	Pints			=	4	Cups
		=	16	Cups			=	32	Ounces
		=	128	Ounces					
1	Cup	=	16	Tablespoons	1	Tablespoon	=	3	Teaspoons
		=	48	Teaspoons					
		=	8	Ounces	1	Pound	=	16	Ounces

Some ingredients, like eggs, are still measured by count, as most chicken eggs are approximately the same size.

COOKING OILS

A great deal of food preparation will require using *cooking oil*, a specially refined form of liquid fat (plant, animal, or synthetic in nature). Oil is useful in the cooking process because it can be heated at much higher temperatures than water and is a better conductor of heat, thereby speeding up the time it takes to cook a dish. It also is helpful in keeping food from sticking to pans and for flavoring purposes.

When selecting the correct cooking oil, consider the type of cooking you will be doing. Many experienced chefs use olive oil, pumice olive oil, or butter for almost all cooking (except frying). Olive oil, traditionally part of the Mediterranean diet, is one of the healthiest fats in the world, containing antioxidants and health-promoting fatty acids.

Also keep in mind that due to high demand for its nutritional benefits, there is a lot of market fraud associated with the olive oil market. Many oils labeled as such, even "extra virgin olive oil," have been mixed with cheaper oils or chemicals. Make sure the brand you select is coming from a reputable supplier (or if you are at a supermarket, look for California Olive Branch, Cobram Estate, or even the Kirkland Signature or Trader Joe's brand[iv] to assure quality. Note that high quality brands need not be overly expensive or even come from the Mediterranean region!).

To further assure the authenticity of your extra virgin olive oil, look for the seal of the California Olive Oil Council (pictured below) on the bottle:

Source: California Olive Oil Council

Butter is the best oil used for browning, or for when you want your dish to have a bit of color.

For frying, canola oil is a great choice. It is very versatile and can also be used for deep frying and making salad dressing. Its smoke point is very high, so it is very stable at high temperatures.

To decide whether a certain oil is suitable for your cooking purposes, be knowledgeable about the oil's *smoke point*, the stage at which heated fats begin to emit smoke and odor. (Note that odors from smoke can seep into the food and these flavors can be very difficult, if impossible, to remove; see the chart on page 46.)

Cooking Oil	Origin	Smoke Point (in ° F)	Uses
Flaxseed oil	Plant	225	Salad dressings, nutritional supplement
Pumpkin seed oil	Plant	250	Salad oils
Butter	Animal	302	Cooking, baking, condiment, sauces, flavoring
Virgin coconut oil	Plant	350	Commercial baking, candies, whipped toppings, creamers (non-dairy), shortening
Unrefined corn oil	Plant	352	Frying, baking, salad dressings, shortening
Extra virgin olive oil	Plant	374	Cooking, salad oils
Lard	Animal	374	Baking, frying
Canola oil	Plant	400	Frying, baking, salad dressings
Grapeseed oil	Plant	400	Cooking, salad dressings
Peanut oil	Plant	450	Frying, cooking, salad oils
Corn oil	Plant	450	Frying, baking, salad dressings, shortening
Soybean oil	Plant	460	Cooking, salad dressings, vegetable oils
Canola oil (high oleic)	Plant	475	Frying, baking, salad dressings

When cooking, make sure that the temperature does not exceed the flash point, the stage at which the vapors of a fluid will ignite. However, you can usually remedy this by removing the source of ignition, such as a cooking pan that is conducting heat, and turning off the heat.

A final note about cooking oils: Always make sure to dispose of used/waste cooking oil in a closed container (a metal can is a good option) in the trash. Do not pour it down a sink drain or in the toilet!

MEATS & FISH

Meats and fish will be among the most popular ingredients served at many restaurants. Meat can be divided into several different cuts. Some of the most popular in the food world are:

1.) ***Filet:*** A boneless cut/ slice of meat or fish.

2.) ***Steak:*** A portion of meat sliced perpendicular to the muscle fibers (though there are exceptions, such as skirt and flank steak in beef).

3.) ***Chop:*** A cut obtained from the area perpendicular to the spine. This usually contains part of a rib or other bone.

4.) ***Ribs:*** Slab-shaped selection of meat attached to the rib bones. Can be served as a rack, where several ribs are separated by hand.

5.) ***Meat on the bone:*** A cut that includes several or all of the bones naturally attached to the meat.

6.) ***Shank:*** A cut from around the lower leg of the animal.

Before you can master the many ways to cook them, you will need to understand some simple information about where cuts of meat come from.

Let's take a look at one of the most popular food animals in America, the cow.

COW

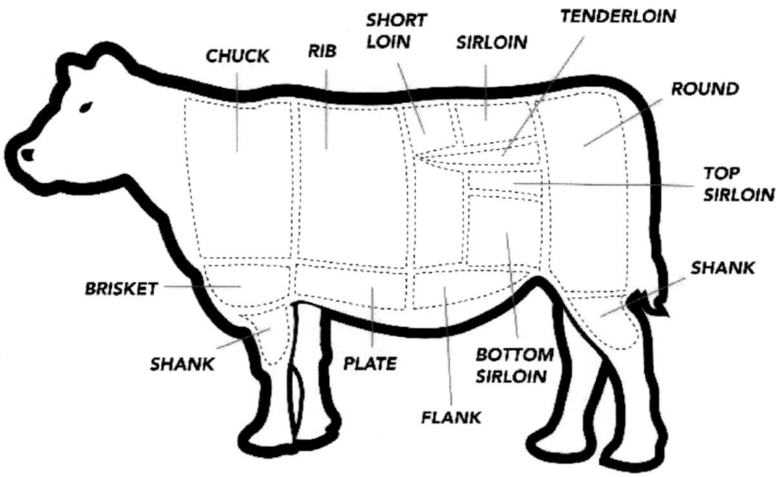

Source: The Kroc Center

We can see in the above diagram where the different cuts of beef originate in the cow. This is an excellent example of how many diverse products can come from the same animal.

See the chart on page 48 for descriptions of the different cuts specific to beef.

Region of Cow	Descriptions/ Uses
Chuck	Mostly muscle, contains connective tissues. Ground beef. Chuck and chuck-eye steak. Flat iron steak. Pot roast meat.
Brisket	Inexpensive, should be slow-cooked. Brisket, corned beef, pastrami.
Shank	Very lean, tends to be tough and dry. Ingredient for soups and stews.
Rib	Most flavorful cut. Grill, broil, saute, or roast. Prime rib, rib roast, ribeye steak.
Plate	Inexpensive, tends to be tough and fatty. Skirt steak, hanger steak, fajita meat, pastrami.
Short Loin	Tender, mild flavor. T-bone steak, Porterhouse steak, strip steak. Broil, saute, or grill.
Flank	Very flavorful and lean. Marinade and/or grill.
Sirloin	"Regular" sirloin steak (usually bone-in), beef loin, flap steak.
Tenderloin	The most tender cuts. Filet mignon, tenderloin steak, Beef Wellington roasts.
Top Sirloin	Top sirloin steak (usually boneless), chateaubriand.
Bottom Sirloin	Less tender than top sirloin, lean, chewy. Flap steak.
Round	Very lean. Top round, London Broil steak. Cook moist or rare.

Though the term "steak" can technically mean a cut from the muscle fibers of any animal, it is most generally used to describe beef. Let's look at the meanings of different terms for steak "doneness:"

Rare—Once cooked (an internal temperature of 125°-130°), a rare steak will be pink on the inside. This allows for the most tender, soft and easy-to-chew end product. *Filet mignon*, a steak originating from the tenderloin region of the animal, is usually served rarer than other beef steaks.

Medium-rare—Has an internal temperature of 130°- 140°. It will have a warm, red center and be firmer than a rare steak. This is usually considered the ideal "doneness" level for beef steaks.

Medium—Has an internal temperature of 140°-150°. The center of the steak will be pink and firm.

Medium-well—Has an internal temperature of 150°-155°. This steak will only have a small amount of pink in the center.

Well-done—Not recommended for steaks, this level of doneness has an internal temperature of over 160°. However, this temperature is just fine for ground beef!

What should you know about cooking beef? Remember the following tips:

- Any cut of beef you select for cooking should be bright red (if kept in a sealed container, it might have a slightly darker color, but will turn red when opened and exposed to the air). If the meat has a tired, pale look, discard it.
- Beef, like most meats, should be defrosted in a refrigerator, not at room temperature.
- Marinating should also be done in a refrigerator, with the meat inside a closed container for 3-24 hours. (Make sure to turn the meat over at approximately the halfway point.)
- When salting beef, it is better to do it after cooking rather than before.

- If you are working with a particularly tough cut (especially one that you plan to cook with high heat), you can opt to use a meat tenderizer. This will resemble a small hammer; pounding slices of the meat will break up the fibers and tissues.

When working with pork (see our pig diagram below), it is also important to know where certain cuts of meat originate from in the animal itself.

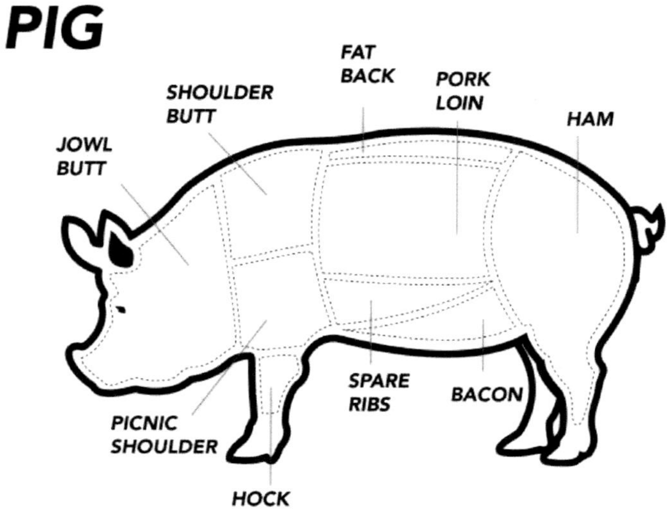

Source: The Kroc Center

An important thing to note in the diagram is that the so-called "butt" portions (sometimes called "Boston butt") actually originate in the shoulder region of the animal, not the rear end. Pork lends itself well to curing, such as in ham and bacon. Pork should be cooked to 150°+.

Source: The Kroc Center

Poultry—primarily chicken (see diagram on previous page) and turkey—are excellent sources of protein and popular in restaurants. Poultry meat comes in "white" and "dark" varieties, with white meat coming from the breast area, and the dark from thighs and leg portions (these are darker in color due to the muscles being used for the sustained activity of walking). Chicken and turkey should be cooked to a temperature of 165°-175°. (Note that animals such as ducks and geese, who often fly for sustained periods, will have dark meat located in their breast regions.)

Another popular meat, especially in Middle Eastern cuisine, is lamb (see diagram below.) This traditionally refers to the meat of a sheep butchered in its first year of life; the meat of an adult sheep is called mutton, with the meat of a juvenile sheep over a year old being hogget (although in the United States, "lamb" can technically refer to the meat of a sheep of any age).

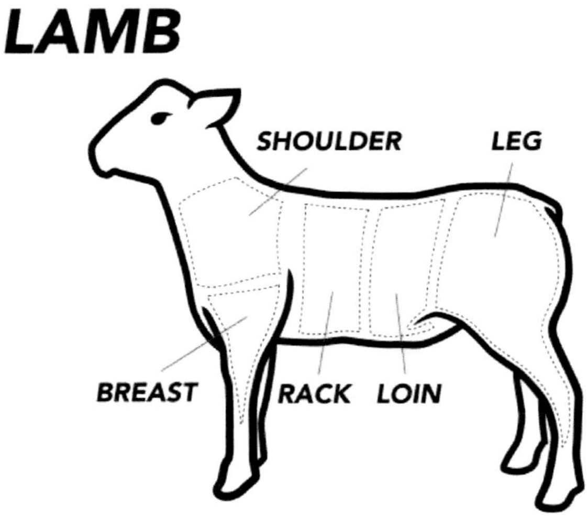

Source: The Kroc Center

Lamb is prized for the tenderness and mild flavor of its meat. When it comes to sheep meat, the darker it is, the older the animal was when slaughtered (young lamb is a pale pink color, while the meat of older sheep run the color gamut to a reddish pink.)

Note that lamb chops can be from the rib, loin, and/or shoulder areas! The ideal "doneness" for lamb is medium-rare, which is an internal termperature of 140°-150°F. Ideally, lamb should be marinated for 4-8 hours.

However, not all meat is created equal just because of came from the same area of the animal! The quality of the meat will depend largely on the quality of the animal it was derived from.

Genetics play a role in this, which is why most farmers are very involed in the breeding of their animals and only select the best of their stock for this purpose. Farmers also pay a premium for animals whose lineage suggests a higher-quality animal.

However, there is also the "nurture" factor along with the "nature" one, which in the case of animals refers to the animal's living situation and environment (more about this in the "Competing Types of Farming Animals for Food" section of this chapter).

When it comes to fish, there are really only a few options to prepare the animal for consumption. First, you will need to remove the organs (including the gills). You can then cook it whole or cut it into the desired shape. Some standard cuts for fish are pictured in the chart on the next page.

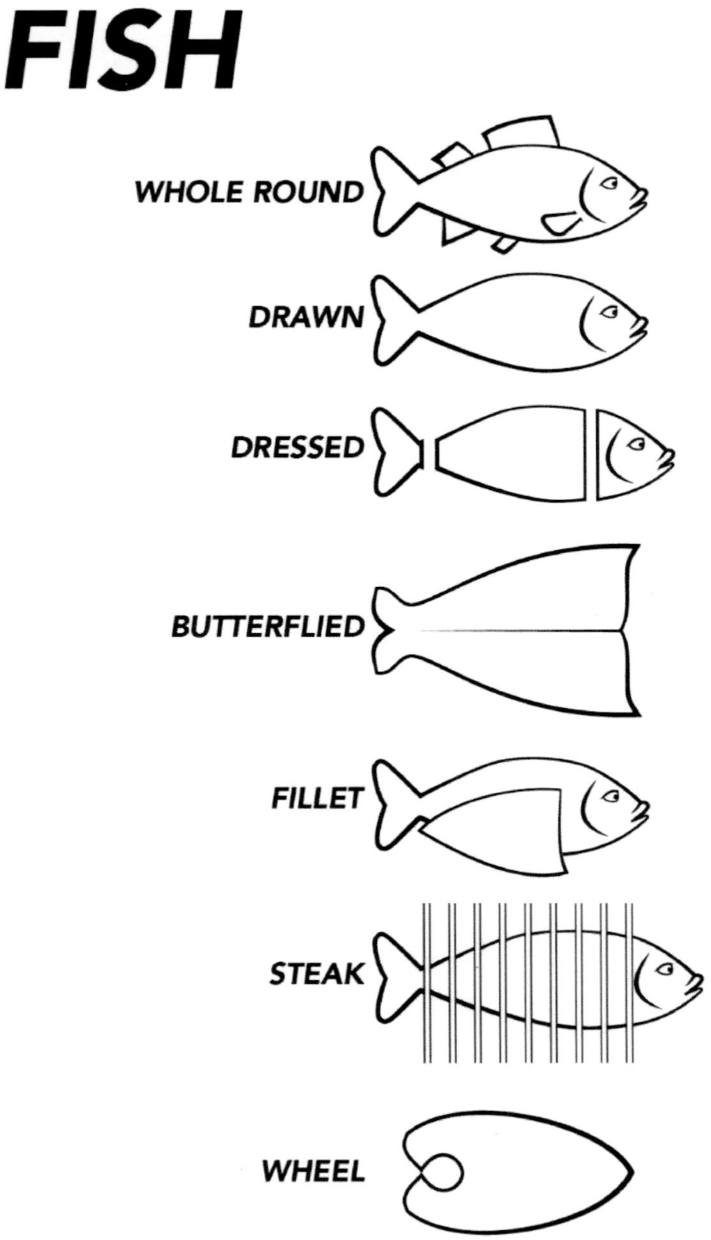

Source: The Kroc Center

Now let's take a look at the anatomy of a fish:

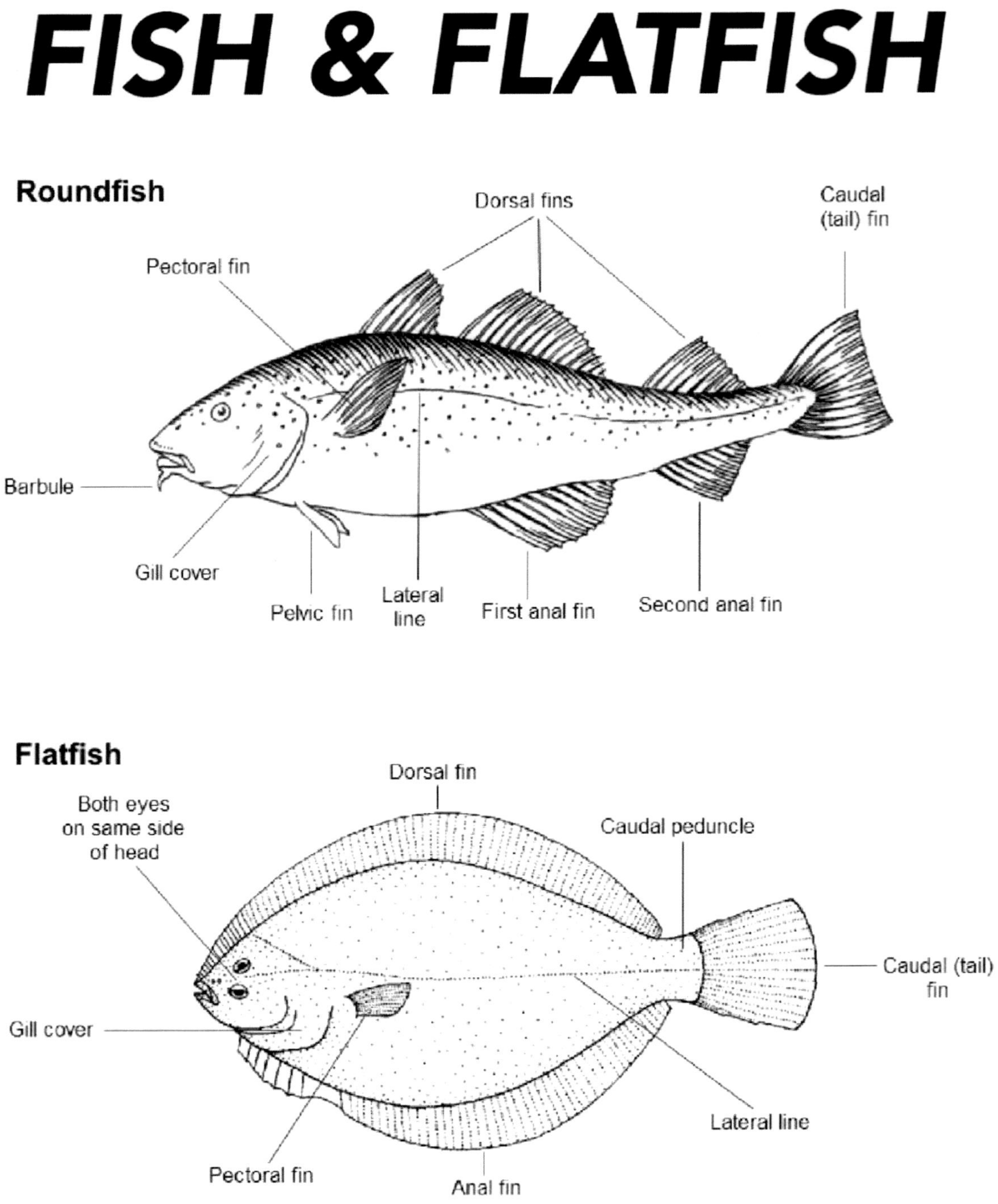

Source: The Kroc Center

(Common types of roundfish include cod, bass, salmon, tilapia, haddock, mackeral, and catfish. Popular flatfish include flounder, sole, and halibut.)

When choosing fish for cooking, it is important to ensure that the meat is fresh. Unless you have caught the fish yourself or were presented with it just after it was caught, you will have to look for telltale signs that the fish is suitable.

The first and most important rule is to smell the fish. Most people immediately recognize the pungent stink of rank, rotting fish. Cooking will not revive or improve spoiled meat, so avoid nasty-smelling specimens at all costs!

If the fish is whole, examine the eyes. Fresh fish have clear and bright eyes; if they are sunken, cloudy and/or dull, the fish is not suitable for cooking! Also make sure that the fish's scales are shiny and metallic-looking, and that the gills are a lively red color. Overall, the fish should present as if it were caught recently. (Note that most grocery stores will debone and/or filet the fish for you if you wish.)

Decoding the freshness of fish fillets is more difficult-- if it passes the smell test, press it with your finger (you can do this even if the fillet has plastic wrap over it). The flesh should be firm and springy, and the indent should disappear presently. Lastly, ensure that there is no milky liquid coming out of the fillet (clear is okay) and that the edges are not turning brown.

Make sure the fish is kept cold until right before it is prepared for consumption (if the fish needs to be stored for a long period of time before being eaten, it is best to freeze it. If the fish needs to sit out for a while after preparation, such as at a buffet, make sure to put it on ice).

Be sure to use separate cutting boards/ food services for the fish and other ingredients you might be preparing at the same time to avoid cross-contamination.

COMPETING TYPES OF FARMING ANIMALS FOR FOOD

When an animal is raised for food purposes, what that animal eats matters because when you consume its meat, you are also consuming the effects of its diet and lifestyle.

Take cows: Almost all calfs are born in spring and are nursed by their mothers for the first months of their lives.

However, if this calf is promised to a large corporation, it usually is shipped off at 6 months to 1 year of age to a *concentrated animal feeding operation*, or CAF. Here, the cows will spend the rest of their days in cramped, unsanitary conditions, being fed a cheap, highly processed mixture of corn and soy products to fatten them up as quickly and efficiently as possible.

To combat the rampant disease that can spread in such conditions, the cows are injected with antibiotics, whose net effect is to "knock out" many of the naturally-occurring and beneficial vitamins that occur in beef (more about that later in this section).

Cows are also injected with many drugs and unnatural hormones to allow their bodies to deal with the effects of their diet and lifestyle. After a few months in the CAF, the cows are sent off to the slaughterhouse for processing as our food.

When we purchase this food at a store or eat it at a restaurant, we are ingesting part of the antibiotics, drugs, and hormones that the animal consumed.

In contrast, let's say calfs grow up on the same farm on which they were born and are allowed to roam more freely, eating grass and naturally-occurring plant life that it encounters in its environment. There is a good reason that cows are referred to as "Nature's lawnmower"—cows love all sorts of plants and greenery is its natural diet.

Once a cow with this lifestyle is slaughtered, its meat will contain fewer calories, gram for gram, than corn-fed beef. (However, the meat will still have a high fat content.)

However, the composition of the fats present in corn-fed and grass-fed meat can be very different. Both corn and grass-fed meat have approximately the same levels of saturated and monosaturated fats. However, the "good" omega-3 fatty acids (also present in many fish, plants, nuts, and seeds) are present in grass-fed meats around *5 times as much* as in the meat from cows who have been corn-fed[v]. Omega-3 is important because it fights against high blood pressure and maybe even Alzheimer's.

Grass-fed beef is also higher in many vitamins, such as vitamin A, vitamin E--an important antioxidant-- and iron. Cows tend to lose their natural stores of these beneficial nutrients the longer they spend in a commercial feed lot.

Human beings are similar to animals in that if they eat a diet high in hormone-treated, highly-processed fast and junk food, they are apt to be less healthy and have a higher vulnerability to obesity, diabetes, and high blood pressure.

The same thing happens to chickens who are housed in cramped, stressful factory conditions where they are are fed an unhealthy diet and treated with hormones to fatten them up as quickly as possible. Eggs derived from these unfortunate animals contain 2-4 times *less* omega-3's than chickens who are raised in more natural conditions[vi]. The eggs also contain higher cholesterol levels than those of naturally- raised birds.

Fish is also a popular meat, as it is high in many vitamins and minerals that keep human beings healthy and fit, including Vitamins A and D (though many fish also contain high levels of mercury, which is especially dangerous for pregnant women and young children to consume.)

It is also common for many types of food fish (including salmon, tilapia, carp, and catfish) to be farmed due to overfishing of these popular species in the wild. Though this increases the supply of fish available for consumption and often drives down prices, farmed fish can often be of inferior quality compared to wild-caught specimens.

This is due to unnatural overcrowding (even for animals that school in the wild) in fish farms and, just like with farmed land animals, a comparatively poor diet and water quality. Parasites and disease can spread easily in these conditions. Fish in farms are often treated with antibiotics and treatments (such as those to make the coloring of their meat more closely resemble wild-caught fish)[vii].

GRADES OF MEAT AND OTHER SEALS

The US government (specifically as the US Department of Agriculture, also known as USDA) has a grading system to inform consumers about the meat they are buying (though some cities and states might have their own unique systems).

Different kinds of meat are graded differently as well. For instance, a component of the grading of beef is the "marbling," or combination of intramuscular fat with the rest of the meat. You will not see this with graded pork or chicken.

The categories are as follows:

Prime: The highest quality meat available, these usually have excellent flavor, texture, and coloring. However, be aware that Prime-graded meats often contain more fat (hence the great flavor), and you will pay for this when you purchase by weight (it is also obviously the most expensive choice). Also note that high-end restaurants usually snap up these meats (only 3% of the general supply) right away, leaving only a small supply for regular consumers.

Choice: The second-highest grade of meat. These meats won't have as much tasty fat as Prime meats and will show slightly less favorable coloring, but is a superior cut for cooking. Still an excellent, tender, and juicy selection!

Good: Meats of this grade are, as the name implies, a "good," middle-of-the-road choice for cooking. Look for a lower ratio of fat to lean meat.

***Standard/ Select*:** This grade designates meat that is acceptable for consumption but definitely not of good quality. Look for poor coloring, texture (not very tender, stringy), and taste.

***Commercial/ Industrial*:** The lowest-quality meat grade. Meats in this category are only suitable for consumption in industrial settings (prisons, schools) where price is far more important than food quality, or for use in large commercial facilities where food is heavily processed.

To recognize a US government grade, look for a seal like on the next page:

You might also see something like that looks like this:

These seals indicate that the product has been inspected by the USDA and were found to pass any regulations, i.e. no dangerous handling or contaminants were detected.

When shopping for organic products, make sure to look for this seal:

This seal certifies that the product has been designated "USDA Organic," an important attestation for food that aspires to call itself by that name. The USDA defines *organic* as food "produced using sustainable agricultural production practices. Not permitted are most conventional pesticides; fertilizers made with synthetic ingredients, or sewage sludge, bioengineering, or ionizing radiation. Organic meat, poultry eggs, and dairy products come from animals that are given no antibiotics or growth hormones."

As you can see, these standards are very strict and consider all matters of supply, production, processing, and distribution. This seal assures the consumer that at least 95% of the product has determined to have been produced via organic means.

(Note that many smaller farms may not pursue USDA Organic certification due to the amount of papework and fees involved. Just because they do not carry USDA certification does not mean that they do not utilize organic practices.)

FRUITS, VEGETABLES, LEGUMES, & GRAINS

Other important diet staples are fruits, vegetables and grains. The most pertinent thing to confirm when working with these is that they are fresh, fresh, fresh! If possible, obtain vegetables that have been picked that day. (Make sure to always wash your vegetables in cold water before using.)

When cooking vegetables, be very careful about overcooking. Vegetables usually do not require a lot of heat or time to cook, and cooking them for even a moment longer than necessary will affect the taste and valuable nutritional content.

For seasoning, adding salt soon after beginning to cook will help retain natural coloring and flavor.

Since most fruits have an abundance of natural sugars, they usually do not need anything added. Fruit is usually served raw, whole or in large chunks, as sides, garnishes, or in a salad.

Of couse all cooks will need to be able to whip up a decent salad! Though preparing a salad is fairly self-explanatory, there are a few rules that need to be followed:

- Always make sure the lettuce and ingredients (including salad dressings!) are fresh.
- Place the head of lettuce in a container of water to ensure its cleanliness before preparing (lettuce from the store or direct from a farm can often be very dirty). Drain the leaves in a colander or put the ingredients through a salad spinner to remove any excess water.
- Chill your greens before preparation.
- Pay attention to the visual colors and competing tastes when mixing a salad.

However, fruits and vegetables that you might want for your dish might not always be in season or easily available. While most restaurants will always prefer the use of fresh ingredients, frozen vegetables and fruit can be substituted.

Frozen fruits and vegetables often employ the IQF (Individually Quick Frozen) method. This means that each small piece of food is frozen separately from all the others, such as in a bag of frozen peas. This makes them much easier to cook with than one large bagged chunk of frozen peas.

Frozen vegetables will often have more nutritional value than canned varieties[viii] due to using cold temperatures rather than artificial chemical preservatives to keep the food fresh. (An exception to this rule is canned tomatoes, whose canning process releases lycopene, an important antioxidant. Note that tomatoes canned in glass jars are preferable to those metal cans.)

As far as grains go, the most common ones include barley, corn, millet, oats, quinoa, rice (wheat and wild), rye, and sorghum. Because grains are brimming with carbohydrates and usually easy to grow and/or inexpensive to purchase, they are diet staples all over the world.

With pastas and bread, want to ensure that the ingredients used are high-quality. Freshly made bread and homemade pasta are always preferred.

When cooking vegetables and pasta, it is important to learn the difference in cooking times for *al dente* (firm to the bite, but thoroughly cooked), *molto al dente* (slightly undercooked), and thoroughly cooked (but not mushy) pasta.

Some foods in these categories have special rules. For instance, after peeling and dicing potatoes or apples, make sure to soak them in cold water. (For apples, add a small amount of fresh lemon juice to retain natural coloring.)

With beans, make sure to sort them for rocks and soak them overnight; this will make them easier to cook. Ideally, you want to cook them in the water they were soaked in until they are tender. (If soaking overnight is not possible, pour cold water over the beans and boil, then cover and set aside for an hour).

Of course, preprocessed beans do not require these steps, but they also have less nutritional value. Keep in mind that beans also expand to twice their size during cooking-- for instance, if you begin with 1 cup of beans, after cooking you will have 2 cups.

When it comes to potatoes, it is especially important to buy organic as they are especially vulnerable to pesticides, many of which inhibit the ability of potato to sprout and are toxic to humans. Because potatoes grow underground, they easily absorb any substances sprayed into the soil.

SAUCES

One of the most popular ways to flavor food and make it uniquely your own is to use a sauce. A successful sauce will enhance and complement the flavors that already exist in a dish.

Any cooking position of note will require you to know the five *mother sauces*, or types of basic sauces which are often used alone, or as the bases for more creative or complex sauces.

A *sauce* is a flavored liquid dressing designed to accompany food that is often made from a *stock.* Stock refers to a strained liquid resulting from cooking vegetables, meat, or fish together with other seasoning ingredients.

Commonly used stocks include chicken, beef, and fish. Many soups and sauces begin with a stock base; for sauces, the stock is usually *reduced*, or cooked down (left to cook and "reduce" via evaporation).

Derived from traditional French cooking, the mother sauces are:

1.) ***Bechamel***- A sauce that milk-based, often thickened with a *roux* (an equal mixture of flour and fat that is cooked together over low heat).

2.) ***Espagnole***-- A brown veal or beef sauce, also often thickened with a roux.

3.) ***Tomato***-- A sauce with a tomato (and sometimes stock) base. This can be as simple as a sauce used with spaghetti.

4.) ***Hollandaise***-- A sauce with a mixture of egg yolks and butter. Most famously, this sauce is used on Eggs Benedict.

5.) ***Veloute***-- A lighter sauce with a white stock base.

Also note that a sauce that is made by enhancing one of the mother sauces with extra ingredients is often called a "daughter sauce" in this tradition.

(See the following pages for recipes for each sauce, which students will practice making in each class. Also take a look at some other cooking terms you will need to know in the chart below.)

Other Cooking Terms

Blanch	*Food is cooked for a very short period of time in boiling water/ hot fat. Most commonly a preparation step to partially cook items such as French fries.*
Deglaze	*Simmering a liquid to remove food particles from the bottom of a pan. Used to pull food off of the bottom to prevent burning.*
Glaze	*Apply a shiny substance to the surface of food, most often with icing or a sauce. This can also be done by melting a substance (i.e. sugar) on top of the food.*
Nappé	*To coat the back of a spoon. Used to check consistency of a soup or sauce.*
Papillote	*Food is wrapped in paper/ foil and steamed to cook.*
Parcook	*Partial cooking of food, by any method.*
Reduce	*To "boil down" a liquid (usually a sauce) by simmering and/or boiling. This method allows the flavors to be concentrated as the liquid is evaporated.*
Sear	*Browning the surface of food quickly via high heat.*
Scorch	*To burn the bottom of a pan that contains food.*
Slurry	*Mixing corn starch and cold water into a peanut butter-like consistency. Used as a thickener for soups or sauce.*
Smoke-Roast	*Cooking with dry heat in the presence of smoke.*
Sous vide	*Refers to food that is cooked while vacuum-packed.*
Sweat	*Cook slowly in fat without browning the food. Usually done in a covered container.*

Bechamel Sauce

Makes 1 cup.

1 cup milk
2 tablespoons butter
2 tablespoons flour
1 small onion studded with 2-3 cloves
1 bay leaf
1 clove
Salt and white pepper to taste

1.) Heat milk in a saucepan over medium heat.
2.) Peel onion. Take bay leaf and pin to the onion with clove to make an onion paquette.
3.) Add onion paquette to milk.
4.) In separate saucepan, melt butter.
5.) Once butter is melted, added flour. Allow to blend for 1-2 minutes, stirring with a wooden spoon until it achieves the consistency of peanut butter. This will now be a white roux.
6.) Once milk comes to a boil, pour over roux.
7.) Whisk all ingredients and cook for 15 minutes or until starch flavor is gone.
8.) Season with salt and white pepper to taste.

Espagnole Sauce

Makes 6 cups.

8 cups beef stock
1 cup mirepoux (mixture of 50% onions, 25% carrots, 25% celery, chopped)
½ cup flour
10 black peppercorns
2 cups crushed tomatoes
½ cup parsley, coarsely chopped
1 cup butter
1 tablespoon apple cider vinegar
Salt and pepper to taste

1.) In a heavy saucepan, melt butter.
2.) Once butter is melted, add mirepoux.
3.) When it begins to brown, add flour. Stir until flour is good and brown.
4.) Add all other ingredients except apple cider vinegar, salt, and pepper.
5.) Bring to a boil, then reduce to a simmer. Cook for 20 minutes.
6.) Strain and adjust flavor to taste with salt and pepper. Add apple cider vinegar.

Hollandaise Sauce

Makes 1 cup.

½ cup butter
1 ½ tablespoons lemon juice, fresh
3 egg yolks
¼ teaspoon salt
Pinch cayenne pepper

1.) In the bottom portion of a double broiler, bring a small amount of water to a boil.
2.) In a separate pan, melt butter slowly over low heat. Set aside but make sure it stays warm.
3.) In a third pan, barely heat lemon juice.
4.) In the top portion of the double broiler, add egg yolks and beat with a whisk.
5.) Add 1 tablespoon boiling water from the bottom of the double broiler to the egg yolks.
6.) Add 2 additional tablespoons boiling water. Continue to beat until the egg yolks thicken.
7.) Add the warmed lemon juice from step 3 and beat.
8.) Remove double broiler from the heat. Beat mixture well with a whisk.
9.) While beating, slowly add butter and cayenne pepper.
10.) Once sauce is thick, serve immediately.

Tomato Sauce

Makes 4 cups.

3 tablespoons olive oil
1 onion, chopped
2 celery ribs, chopped
1 carrot, chopped
1 garlic clove
4 cups crushed tomatoes
2 teaspoons each of thyme, basil, rosemary, chopped
1 teaspoon salt
½ teaspoon pepper
2 tablespoons balsamic vinegar

1.) Over low heat, combine olive oil, onions, celery ribs, carrot, and garlic clove in a saucepan. Cook for 3 minutes, stirring.
2.) Add crushed tomatoes.
3.) Cook sauce uncovered for 45 minutes, or until thick.
4.) Add herbs, salt, and pepper, and balsamic vinegar while still hot.

VELOUTE SAUCE

Makes 2 cups.

½ cup butter
½ cup flour
2 ½ cups chicken, veal, or fish stock
1 tablespoon apple cider vinegar
Nutmeg, salt, and pepper to taste

1.) In a saucepan, melt butter.
2.) Once melted, stir in flour. Blend.
3.) Once blended well, gradually add stock. Stir well over low heat.
4.) Once blended and thickened, bring to a boil. Simmer for 20 minutes, stirring occasionally.
5.) Remove from heat and strain. Add apple cider vinegar. Salt, pepper, and nutmeg to taste.

SPECIAL DIETS

Another situation that any chef or food service worker will face is preparing dishes for those on special diets. Please see the table below, which gives general guidelines on some of the most common diets.

Types of Diets

Name	Forbidden!
Paleo/ Caveman	Starches Beans Corn Sugar Dairy Grains Processed foods
Vegetarian	Meats
Raw food	Meats Cheese Dairy Processed foods Anything cooked 118°
Gluten-Free	Grains Starches Breads
Kosher	Seafoods Meats and cheeses together Pork
Vegan	Dairy Meats Eggs

A chef might want to keep these in mind when preparing a menu, as ideally all diners would be able to consume at least one dish from the restaurant menu (this does not apply if the restaurant itself caters to a special population).

BONUS SECTION: FOOD AS MEDICINE

AN INTERVIEW WITH MYRON HARDESTY

One of Chef Timothy Tucker's strongest personally-held beliefs that he tries to pass on to students is the concept of food as medicine. Quite simply, this is the notion that eating well and proper nutrition, with knowledge and mindfulness, can maintain optimal health and, if necessary, heal the body.

Myron Hardesty is a licensed physician assistant and medical herbalist who has been practicing for almost twenty years. He currently runs an apothecary in Louisville, Kentucky called Weeds of Eden. He has been asked to answer a few questions for this book that will hopefully be beneficial in explaining this topic. (The interview has been edited for length and clarity.)[ix]

Q: You have training in both traditional (e.g. modern) medicine and natural medicine. How did you become convinced of the medical value of natural or alternative medicine?

A: I was sick myself when I was younger. I had cat scratch fever, which is a bacterial infection-- that they supposed at the time was transferred by cats, but can actually be transmitted in lots of different ways...

It wasn't until I went out west, to Boulder, Colorado, that I saw an herbalist who basically told me that my lymphatic system was screwed up, and that there are herbs you can take that would help decongest the lymph system, and… I didn't have lymphatic swelling after I went to this herbalist. She taught me [about] the plants of the region, and the fact that I was using some of those plants to heal myself was just a revolutionary thought to me… It went through my head that this was something I wanted to pursue for the rest of my life.

Q: Why did you feel the need to be trained as a medical assistant after you began your career in natural medicine?

A: After I opened my shop and ran it for a number of years, I realized that a number of [my patients'] issues were actually due to side effects of drugs, in which case there wasn't a natural therapy, per se, to properly treat them. Eventually, I would just print out information about the person's medication and highlight side effects for [the client] and then send them back to their doctor. Anything I could do would only be a Band-Aid.

I got interested and realized that if I wanted to provide truly proactive medicine… I would have to get a [medical] license. That is what really prompted me to go back to school because I really love all aspects of medicine… [And] it used to frustrate me that I didn't know much about the pharmacological effects of herbs.

Q: Do you feel there are times where modern medical treatment has harmed the patient, and that you could have healed them more efficiently if you had gotten to them first?

A: Absolutely. [Taking good care of your body] most of the time it is like tending the soil in your garden—making sure it is adequately nutrified and has everything it needs in order to perform its vital functions.

Generally, people poo-poo the concept of nutrition or natural medicine because it is so poorly taught in the [modern] medical model, but you can see that we are transforming our food supply, and this leads to transforming ourseslves. Sometimes I wish that I were given the opportunity to build [the patient] up before they undergo a harsh therapy like chemotherapy or surgery.

Q: What is the difference between preventative maintenance and trying to heal the body after the fact?

A: Preventive maintenance is easier and saves a lot more money! When it comes to chronic diseases, so much of the treatment available is based on the miracles of antibiotics and surgery, that are undeniably progressive. However, the landscape of illness in modern America has shifted from these acute infections or war injury issues, to dealing with chronic disease states like obesity or diabetes. We are living in an old paradigm of care that is not premised on preventive care, and [the need] to get back to basic nutrition and prevention of chronic disease is more crucial.

Q: What advice would you give to my students on things they can do daily to assist with preventive maintenance?

A: So, one has to start with the idea that we are in nutritional freefall in America. We have been stripmining the topsoil for eons, to the point where we are not getting the nutrients our ancestors got… [That natural] food chain has been broken through use of pesticides and bacteria and fungal ecosystems, and broken in our own digestive tracts because of antibiotics.

Once you accept that as a clinical reality, I would recommend food-grown vitamins, omega-3 fatty acids from organic sources like fish, Vitamin D (as our modern lifestyle often doesn't allow us to get enough), and magnesium because it the most pronounced nutrient deficiency today.

Q: Would these be available in a regular multivitamin?

A: Sometimes, but be sure to check the labels. The type and amounts of vitamins a person needs depends on many factors such as where the patient lives, their lifestyle, and what their genetic makeup is. There isn't a one-size-fits-all solution.

Q: Why do you feel that natural medicine is sometimes not well-regarded within the larger medical community?

A: I think it boils down to the fact that here in America, we have commercialized our medicine to the point where the industry is patent-driven. Since you can't patient natural medicine, there is no incentive to finance studies on herbs, and you need many studies for anything to be approved by the FDA.

So we have a situation where it is not affordable to do real scientific research, and this leads to rampant hucksterism in the natural medicine industry. There are a lot of shoddy, poor quality products out there. For instance, if you see the term "proprietary blend" on the label, you cannot tell how much of the listed ingredients—which could be legimately useful ingredients for the complaint-- are actually in what you're taking. Maybe there are only microamounts of the active ingeredient, and the cheapest ingredient is most of the content of the product.

Q: What should we look for as consumers?

A: It comes down to who picks the herbs, who manufactures the product, and who turned it to into medicine. I want to get as close to the earth as possible—How was it grown? Was it grown organically?

So it really comes down to relationships and how much you know about that product. It comes down to developing relationships with your farmer, your pharmacist, your cook, and your chef; it comes down to trust and knowing people's standards.

For further information on ingredients that heal various ailments, see the chart on the next page.

Ingredient	Ideal Cure for...
Garlic (Raw)	Colds, lowering blood pressure
Ginger (raw, fresh)	Burns (press onto burned area for 15 mins.), stomachache
Lavender oil	Disinfectant (cuts and burns)
Cloves	Toothache (crush buds and hold on ache), nausea
Lemongrass	Colds
Cranberry	Urinary tract infections
Tumeric	Liver cleanser, antifungal, antiviral, lowers blood cholesterol, heals wounds
Borage	Depression and stress (tea)
Basil	Indigestion, stress, tension headaches
Cayenne pepper	Stimulates and purifies blood, decreases swelling
Burdock root	Removes toxins, skin problems (eczema, acne), digestive system
Lysine	Cold sores
Cardamom (seeds)	Appetite stimulation, improves nutrient absorption
Cumin (seeds)	Diuretic
Dill seeds	Bad breath
Echinacea	Infections in respiratory and digestive system
Fenugreek	Reduces blood sugar levels, menstrual pain
Hyssop	Cold sores, mild pain reliever and diuretic
Licorice root	Gentle laxative, anti-inflammatory, detoxifies, regulates blood sugar, peptic ulcers, sore throats
Nutmeg	Anti-inflammatory
Parsley	Antioxidant, diuretic
Rose petal	Antioxidant, diuretic, antiseptic
Sage	Antioxidant, antimicrobial, antibiotic, antiseptic
Thyme	Antioxidant, heals wounds, antiseptic, calms coughs
Cinnamon	Nausea, vomiting, diarrhea, antimicrobial

3. Recipes

"A recipe is a story that ends with a good meal."

--Pat Conroy

Anyone who has any experience with cooking has probably had to read and follow a recipe at some point.

Whether it was a handwritten recipe passed down in the family through generations or something downloaded from the Internet, recipes are maps written to guide the reader through the creation of a culinary masterpiece.

Therefore, it is essential to know how to read, interpret, and cook from a recipe.

On the following page, you will see a favorite recipe of Chef Timothy's:

Bourbon & Green Garlic Kentucky Short Ribs

Makes 4 servings.

1 ¼ cup soy sauce
1 ¼ cup teriyaki sauce
1 cup honey
1 cup molasses
1 whole stalk green garlic (or 1 whole clove garlic)
1 onion, quartered
1 green pepper, seeded and quartered
1 (2 x 2 inch) piece fresh ginger, peeled and thinly sliced
1 ½ cups beer
¾ cup Kentucky bourbon
½ cup fresh Thai basil
¼ cup chili garlic sauce
2 tablespoons malt vinegar
2 lbs. Kentucky-raised beef short ribs
Salt and pepper (to taste)

1.) In a 4 quart slow cooker, mix together all ingredients except the ribs..
2.) Heat a large skillet and add oil. Season ribs with salt and pepper. Sear ribs until golden brown.
3.) Add ribs to the slow cooker. Cook for 5 hours at 200 degrees. When done, the ribs will be very tender and break apart easily.

The first thing to do when you get a recipe is to read it in its entirety. This way you can get an idea of the process the recipe is outlining, from start to finish. Think of the recipe like a short story: there is a beginning that introduces you to the characters: the ingredients and the secific way they need to be prepared. There is a middle: the action part, where the preparation of the dish takes place. At the end, you should have a finished product, and everyone should live happily ever after!

The second thing to do is collect and prepare the ingredients according to the instructions. For instance, to follow our short ribs recipe, it isn't enough to just have an onion and a green pepper. These items need to be prepared for use by quartering, and seeding and quartering, respectively. These actions should be completed *before* we start actually cooking the dish.

Another important thing to remember about preparing the ingredients to create this dish is to ensure you have all the items mentioned in the numbered instructions.

For instance, this recipe calls for a 4-quart slow cooker and a large skillet in addition to the edible ingredients. It would be terrible to begin following the instructions, only to find out that we don't have some of the tools. That's why it's so important to read the whole recipe as our first step!

Additionally, this recipe requires that w mix the ingredients in a slow cooker. So, we will need the proper utensils to perform this task. As you recall from our chapter on Kitchen Equipment, the appropriate tool to use would be a wooden spoon.

Once we are sure we have all the ingredients, food and non-food, we are ready to start cooking!

When making the dish, make sure you are following the proper terms and techniques, e.g. sauté vs. baking vs. frying.

Also pay attention to *how long* and at *what temperature* you are cooking the food. Scorching or burning food can be one of the most difficult cooking mistakes to correct. Once the mistake is made, the taste is often there to stay and will permeate the rest of your dish. However, if you catch yourself early enough in the process, you may be able to simply switch pots/ pans.

RECIPE SUBSTITUTIONS

Occasionally it will become necessary to make substitutions in a recipe. This can be either because the servings the recipe makes is too much/ not enough for your purposes, or because you might not have all the specific ingredients that the recipe calls for.

The recipe for short ribs at the beginning of this chapter calls for a whole stalk of green garlic. However, this was written by a chef living in Louisville, Kentucky-- an area with a burgeoning restaurant scene, a mild climate, and access to some spectacular local farmer's markets.

A person living in an urban area without ready access to fresh produce (or *food desert*) or someone trying to purchase this item offseason would probably have to make a substitution due to the preferred ingredient not being available.

(A note about green garlic: This refers to the tops of garlic bulbs that bloom in late June, which are milder in flavor than regular garlic and have a similar color to green onions. They have a very short season, when it is available at all. In recipes that call for green garlic, a bulb of regular garlic is easily substiuted at the same amount. However, keep in mind that the more it is cooked, the more the flavor will be dulled.)

Note that a substitution of the more common clove of garlic has been suggested. However, most recipes will not be so generous, and the flavor expertise and ingenuity of a cook will be needed.

Aside from the ingredients themselves, you might also need to adjust amounts. Say that you need to make 12 servings of a dish for which you only have a recipe that makes 4 servings. In this case, the student will be instructed to "make 3 times" the recipe.

This is because you will need to multiply each ingredient by 3, as well as making sure that you have the correct sizes of pans and pots, and other kitchen equipment to handle the larger amounts.

However, it would be much easier to multiply the amounts of ingredients in your recipe if you understand that 16 tablespoons are equal to one cup. (Please consult the chart in Chapter 3 to make your math a little easier to cook with!)

Many students ask me why several cooks, following the same recipe, will still end up with slightly different dishes. One of the explanations for this is the use of different ingeredients. Common ingredients, such as soy sauce, will usually be available in many different brands, all of which have their own unique qualities and compositions, and which are themselves prepared using a unique recipe.

Even main ingredients like beef differ. When possible, it is always best to look for the terms "antibiotic-free," "grass-fed," "organic," and the like. As covered in our Food Basics chapter, cows that are grass-fed will produce beef with a cleaner taste than that of cows that are corn-fed and injected with antibiotics.

This is why it is so important to begin with fresh, high-quality ingredients. No matter your skill, a dish prepared with subpar ingredients will never taste its best, even if you follow the recipe carefully.

However, sometimes not having access to the correct ingredient in a recipe is a matter of location. When people move to a different part of the world, or even a different part of the country, access to their preferred ingredient might change, and it might become necessary to substitute brands or ingredients.

Food allergies is another issue that could make substitution necessary. When serving lactose-intolerant folks, using coconut or soy milk instead of cow's milk will still allow you to cook the dish without altering the end product significantly.

You could also use tofu in place of meat in almost any dish if you would like to serve a vegetarian meal, though keep in mind that you will need to cook tofu differently than a cut of meat.

For ingredients like spices and seasonings, fresh herbs are usually preferable to dried herbs. At any given time, a serious cook will have at least 15 varieties of fresh herbs available in the kitchen/ classroom. A good rule of thumb is that the fresh herbs go in at the end of the cooking process, and dried herbs go in at the beginning.

Another advantage is that fresh herbs are assured of having a premium flavor, whereas dried herbs tend to lose their flavor and potency after about three months (though they will still be useful for medicinal qualities).

For dishes like fruit salad, you will need to know how to skillfully combine whatever fruits happen to be in season at the time. Make sure to pay attention to the harmony of flavors *and* colors. After all, if a dish looks good, it leads people to expect that it will also taste good!

SALT: A CHEF'S MISUNDERSTOOD BEST FRIEND

In recipes, you will often see salt listed as an ingredient, with the amount designated as "to taste" (also abbreviated as *T.T.*). This means to add it at your own discretion and using your own judgement.

Salt is one of the most necessary ingredients in cooking and is used both for its own distinctive taste, as well as to bring out the other flavors in a dish. Use of salt will really make the sweetness and acidity in food pop, and the most aromatic and richest flavors cannot be produced properly without it.

In all the previous Culinary Art Training Program classes, there is at least one student who is hesitant to cook with salt, or will only deign to use it in tiny amounts. This is usually because they have heard that salt negatively affects your health (specifically, that it leads to higher blood pressure) and that one should consume as little of it as possible.

Though there is some correlation between high salt consumption and higher blood pressure[x], salt itself is a healthy, natural ingredient and cooking without it can be paralyzing.

Classically-trained chefs have all been taught to be experts at adding the correct amount of salt to a dish, and no respectable chef will run a salt-free kitchen.

In fact, while eating at a fine dining restaurant you might notice that there are no salt and pepper shakers on the tables. This is the chef's way of telling you that s/he has prepared the food to perfection-- including the seasoning-- and there should be no need to add anything. Asking for salt or other condiments might even be interpreted as an insult!

However, for those still worried about salt, sea salt is a good alternative as it has undergone less refining overall than most other types of salt. But keep in mind that it is less powerful than other salts, so you will need to add more than you would if you were using traditional salt.

WHY DOESN'T MY DISH TASTE LIKE ONE FROM THE STORE?

People will often approach a culinary instructor or chef with a storebought product they like, asking how to reproduce it. While the professional may be able to give a recipe that is close to the product they presented, this might not be entirely possible. Why is this?

One answer is that, for obvious reasons, companies will not want to make their recipes public.

But another part of the answer lies in the ingredients that go into a commercial food product versus one you'd prepare in a kitchen for immediate consumption. Let's look at the ingredient list of a Trader Joe's tortilla: flour, niacin, iron, riboflavin, folic acid, malted barley flour, high oleic sunflower oil, etc. There are about 15 ingredients used to make this, many more than if we were to make a tortilla from scratch or from a family recipe!

This is because this tortilla was built for shelf life (at least 2 weeks) and to last through transport to the location of the grocery store. Therefore, preservatives such as citric acid (which raises the acidity) will be used.

Vinegar, honey, sugar, and chemical additives have also been added to ensure flexibility of a tortilla that must taste fresh far into its life.

Of course, this means that authenticity of ingredients and simplicity of preparation has been the casualty of the model. If we make a tortilla at home the shelf life will only be about two days.

Most home cooks do not use the chemical ingredients used for a grocery store or chain restaurant recipe as they do not need to calculate shelf life into their dish.

So don't expect your homemade dish to keep or taste identical to a storebought dish!

USING RECIPES IN DIFFERENT ROLES: THE RECIPE VS. CREATIVITY IN COOKING

There are many ways of looking at a recipe. If you are an inexperienced beginner in the kitchen, you might want to look at a recipe as gospel and strictly follow it to the letter, changing absolutely nothing.

However, for the creative cook, it can be a loose template, or starting point, for a creation that will highlight that particular individual's specific tastes and culinary background.

A natural question when looking at a recipe is: How closely do I have to follow it *really*?

Aside from depending on your level of experience, the answer could also depend on your job: For instance, are you an executive chef with your own restaurant or a line cook at a corporate chain?

Recipes are often interpreted loosely, if they are consulted at all, for the creative chef. They feel free to substitute ingredients here, and cooking methods there. However, they also have the necessary know-how and experience to ensure that the dish turns out as they have envisioned.

But let's pretend that you have a job working in a restaurant as a line or prep cook. Yes, you are being paid to prepare food, but you are not being paid to be a culinary innovator. You are expected to follow the recipe as is, to ensure that the chef's vision for every dish turns up as perfectly as possible on every plate, every time.

This is also particularly true when working in a corporation-owned casual dining food restaurant such as Chili's, Applebees, or Olive Garden. To make sure that the food at every chain location tastes exactly the same, the food is often prepared in a commissary kitchen, or an industrial location where food is prepared in huge quantities for commercial interests. The food is then frozen or otherwise packaged for transport to the various locations it serves. Many different restaurants, establishments, and food trucks may use the same commissary kitchen.

One of the reasons that I don't recommend that my students work in a chain restaurant like this is that the taste and quality of the food is often sacrificed in the name of cost-effectiveness and a long shelf life (the food here is often chock-full of flavor-killing preservatives, to make sure that it does not spoil in storage). If someone is at all interested in cooking real food, you can see how choosing this line of work would be very limiting.

Additionally, the restaurant work here is often assembly-based, rather than cooking-based. Sure, you will need to have basic knife skills and santitation know-how, but pay is usually low as it does not require any creativity, a finely tuned palette, or education.

Most corporate restaurant chains have standardized recipes, but also move a lot of product that has been previously frozen. For example, Applebees' soups are made at a plant, then packaged, frozen, and delivered to all the locations that plant serves so that all employees in an Applebees kitchen must do is heat it up. And heating things up is not cooking!

Furthermore, pay is usually at about minimum wage or very close to that.

However, I am not looking to bash any restaurants or indicate that employees at corporate chains do not work hard! In fact, due to heavy volume those workers usually find themselves working as hard or harder than those in fine dining. However, their work is often looked upon as manual labor rather than cooking.

Pay and skills needed are generally comparable, even at a corporate "casual dining" restaurant: Olive Garden, Chilis, or a casual fast food restaurant like Chipotle. Tasks required are still mostly assembly-based. There might not be an actual chef on staff, but rather a kitchen manager, who is more concerned with inventory, purchasing, and enforcing cleanliness standards than cooking. The creative side of cooking is usually not highlighted.

Dishes served at these establishments are usually the creation of a corporate chef. A corporate chef is usually employed at the corporate office for a chain, working out of a test kitchen. S/he creates dishes using market research and pre-approved ingredients that the chain might already have access to to create "new" dishes. Trends, marketing, and mass production are highlighted. And of course all dishes suitable for the chain must be chockful of preservatives and chemicals to ensure safe transport to all of the restaurant locations and storage thereafter, previously mentioned.

On the other hand, line cooks at an authentic restaurant (locally/ privately owned, "mom and pop") must demonstrate real culinary skills as there is little mass-produced food to rely upon.

In this environment, it is still important for a cook to follow recipes faithfully and to turn out consistent dishes.

One of the reasons that chain restaurants are so popular is that customers know that no matter which specific location they choose, the dishes will always taste exactly the same.

Though such strict control does not exist in non-chain restaurants, consistency is still important to run a successful restaurant, which means recipes still play a significant role.

Recipe substitution will be necessary more often, as local restaurants cannot often count on corporate-managed supply chains and are more affected by seasonal ingredients. If the restaurant makes food from scratch, the potential for food waste (see Chapter 6) is also high, so keeping costs under control will be key in this environment.

Though there is often more room for creativity, the top vulnerability for young cooks wanting to be creative is disappointing or confusing the customer who wants an exact replica of the dish they may have eaten before. To avoid this and let their ingenuity run free, cooks should aim to gather the necessary experience and knowhow to become an executive or sous- chef, or even own their own restaurant.

High end restaurants owned by a chef usually highlight more of a passion for food. The clientele is typically very appreciative of creativity and innovation and more knowledgeable about the culinary process.

However, many people choose to circumvent the usually lengthy amount of time it can take to rise through the ranks by becoming a personal chef or caterer, where you are totally in control. However, consistency with dishes is still important!

The fundamentals and tools are still needed to ensure you know what you're doing with cooking and creating good food.

For instance, every baker knows that baking often requires following a recipe precisely. This is due to the process of baking being more unforgiving of mistakes. Many complex chemical processes go into creating baked goods, and you cannot interrupt the process due to making a mistake.

Substitutions are often more difficult here as well, as exact ratios of exact ingredients are needed in order to create the reaction you are looking for. Remember a particularly useful quote by Laiko Bahrs, a professional culinary consultant:

"When baking, follow directions. When cooking, go by your own taste." (More about this below.)

A BASIC BAKING METHOD

Since this book focuses on cooking, we have tried to limit many comments on baking. However, baking is also an important component of working in many professional kitchens.

In general, successful baking comprises much more precise math than cooking does! Bakers use a special notation method to calculate the amounts of ingredients needed to make a certain amount of product; this is called the *baker's percentage*. This math can take the place of a recipe for a baker.

When using the baker's percentage method, each ingredient, including the liquids, is precisely weighed (make sure your ingredients scale is calibrated and working properly). Flour is always expressed as 100% (yes, the end result should be over 100%!), while the weights of the other ingredients are said to be percentages relating to the weight of the flour. Weights are usually calculated using the metric system to make the calculations easier.

For instance, say we need 500 grams (or 1.1 pounds) of flour for a recipe. The flour is expressed as 100% as a baker's percentage. We also need 15 grams of yeast, 860 grams of water and 10 grams of salt. (For baker's math purposes, make sure that all the ingredients are weighed using the same unit of measurement—in this case, grams).

Therefore, the yeast is expressed as 3%, the water as 72%, and the salt as 2%. Note that we are dividing each by 500, the weight of the flour. We are then multiplying that result by 100 to obtain a percentage.

Your final table will look like this:

Ingredient	Amount Needed	Equation Needed	Baker's %age
Flour	500 grams	None	100%
Yeast	15 grams	(15/500) x 100	3%
Water	360 grams	(360/500) x 100	72%
Salt	10 grams	(10/500) x 100	2%

There are also handy online webpages and calculators that can help you with these often inconvenient mathematical needs (for example, to convert units of measurement, try Googling "cups to grams" or "ounces to grams" to access their handy online calculator).

Baking with this method also makes it easier to adjust the amounts needed to increase or downsize the recipe you currently have, according to the yield, or amount of end product, you need. The baker's percentages should give you the answers you need!

For the purposes of this book, I have included a simple bread baking recipe from the New York Times (below)[xi]. This will yield a 1.5 lb loaf.

NO-KNEAD EASY BREAD RECIPE

Baking Time: 24 hours

3 cups all-purpose or bread flour, more for dusting
¼ teaspoon instant yeast
1 ¼ teaspoons salt
Cornmeal or wheat bran as needed

1.) In a large bowl combine flour, yeast and salt. Add 1 5/8 cups water, and stir until blended (dough should be shaggy and sticky).
2.) Cover bowl with plastic wrap. Let dough rest 12-18 hours, at warm room temperature.
3.) Determine if dough is ready to be used: Check if the surface is dotted with bubbles.
4.) Lightly flour a work surface and place dough on it. Sprinkle a little more flour on the dough and fold it over on itself once or twice. Cover loosely with plastic wrap and let rest about 15 minutes.
5.) Using just enough flour to keep dough from sticking, gently and quickly shape dough into a ball. Generously coat a cotton towel (not terry cloth) with flour, wheat bran or cornmeal.
6.) Place dough seam side down on towel and dust with more flour, bran, or cornmeal. Cover with another cotton towel and let rise for about 2 hours. (When it is ready, dough will be more than double in size and will not readily spring back when poked with a finger.)
6.) While dough is rising, heat oven to 450 degrees. Put a 6- to 8-quart heavy covered pot (cast iron, enamel, Pyrex or ceramic) in oven as it heats.
7.) When dough is ready, carefully remove pot from oven. Slide your hand under towel and turn dough over into pot, seam side up; it is okay if it is messy. Shake pan once or twice if dough is unevenly distributed; it will straighten out as it bakes.
8) Cover with lid and bake 30 minutes, then remove lid and bake another 15 to 30 minutes, until loaf is beautifully browned. Cool on a rack.

4. Food Ordering & Storage

"The process and organization leading up to cooking the egg can tell you a lot about the cook."

--David Chang

It's plain to see that being able to cook and prepare delicious food is a significant part of being a culinary professional. But let's not forget how crucial organization and maintenance of your product is, as well as actually obtaining your ingredients!

One of the most important tasks of a cook at any facility is receiving orders of food and supplies. Typically, shipments will be arriving daily, often early in the morning before management and front-of-the-house staff arrive. Line cooks, dishwashers, or anyone responsible and working in the back of the house could be chosen to receive orders.

The most important thing to do when receiving is to inspect the shipment. Make sure that:

- *The product is what you ordered.* Do not accept oranges if you have ordered clementines, or flank steak if you have ordered prime rib. Pay attention to brand names as well if your establishment has a preference.

Suppliers, even reputable ones, can make mistakes and some will even try to send an inferior product or something they have an overstock of in place of what was actually ordered. You are the first line of defense to make sure this has not happened!

- *The product is of adequate quality.* Check any produce carefully for bruises, discolorations, or other markers of poor condition. For meats and other perishables, check expiration dates.

If the delivery person leaves you with a shipment of substandard apples that you sign for, your establishment is usually on the hook for the cost because it was not properly inspected by staff. **Signing your name for the delivery is signing an agreement that everything is fine with the sale**. It will be difficult to convince the supplier later that everything was not received in good order, as something could have happened to the goods after they delivered it, when they are no longer responsible. Of course, it is important to have a trustworthy vendor lined up! But it is **always** important to inspect your shipment and report problems immediately.

- *If problems are noted with the shipment, make sure to show the delivery person the specific source of your complaint and have him/ her sign off that the delivery was deficient.* Otherwise, disagreements later could damage your relationship with your supplier.

Once you sign for a successful delivery, the next step is to put the product away. Every kitchen is organized differently, but should have an assigned place for everything.

While you are putting things away, make a note to inform the chef or sous-chef of any ingredients that are diminishing or almost out. Since they will usually be doing the ordering, it is important for them to have this information.

PROPER FREEZER & DRY FOOD STORAGE

Once received, food must be promptly stored to avoid spoilage and ensure maximum shelf life. Meats and other perishables are stored in a *walk-*

in freezer. A walk-in freezer is a refrigerator the size of a room that stores a wide array of foodstuffs. The temperature should be logged daily and kept at or below 41°F at all times.

During inspections, the health department will pay special attention to the condition of the walk-in freezer. Inappropriate storage can result in fines or even the closing of your establishment.

To avoid this and maintain a satisfactory walk-in, observe the following:

- *The rule of* first in, first out *(FIFO)*. You might have observed this rule in action at the grocery store, where the newest and freshest product will be located at the back of the shelf, while the oldest will be towards the front. Simply put, this means older food should always be used first. Therefore, you will want to stock your freezer in a similar manner, where the oldest product is at the front-- easy to grab for cooking-- while the newest is in the back.

- *Make sure everything is properly wrapped*. Usually, this means an airtight plastic wrap (I recommend a technique called the New York Wrap, where the wrapping is folded underneath the food) over all openings in a container. Storage in a plastic or glass container rated for freezer use can also be used.

I usually do not recommend using aluminum foil, as many ingredients can cause it to degrade (such as tomato-based dishes, whose acidity will cause the foil to deteriorate). However, plastic wrap is usually safe for all foods, as are plastic and glass.

Another thing to avoid is placing metal cans of opened food in the freezer. A metallic flavor may leach into the food, and could even cause food poisoning. Contents of a metal can should be removed to a plastic or glass container and appropriately covered.

Egg dishes left in the fridge overnight must have milk or cream added to them-- especially when stored in an aluminum pan-- or they will turn green due the chemical reaction that takes place between the food and the pan (this is where the term "green eggs and ham" comes from!).

- *Date and label everything!* If your product is not already dated by the manufacturer or supplier, you should always be sure to mark it yourself. Nothing undated should be in the freezer, as this leads to later confusion about freshness and therefore, unnecessary waste.

Always have a black marker and extra plastic/ glass containers on hand!

Checking and managing the contents of the walk-in freezer on a daily basis is also essential, as you want to have a good idea of your inventory levels, and what ingredients you do and do not have.

(Tip: Make sure not to put lettuce or any creamy sauces (as they will curdle or separate) in the freezer! Coffee should also never be stored in a freezer-- a refrigerator is preferred.)

Additionally, as various kitchen staff add contents to the freezer, food can get disorganized, lost, forgotten about, and spoiled. This hurts your budget and creates food waste.

Quality also suffers the longer frozen food is stored. Follow the guidelines below to stay within food safety guidelines (providing that the food is correctly stored; air coupled with moisture is the enemy of frozen food, resulting in freezer burn) but be aware that the food will not be as tasty as it was originally:

Stews, soups, casseroles: 2-3 months

Cooked meats that are not poultry: 2-3 months

Cooked poultry: 4 months

Uncooked poultry: 9-12 months

Any ingredient stored in the freezer after two days should have a plan in place to either use it in a dish or dispose of it. Managing leftovers is paramount to maximizing your budget and keeping up with cleanliness, especially as the freezer can contain fruits and vegetables.

Chefs can find creative ways to use up leftovers, i.e. using the leftover fish from last night's special in a fish stew for tonight.

Dry storage is also an area where the rule of first in, first out should be followed. Flours should be well-wrapped and stored, preferably on a higher shelf, to avoid rodents. Putting out peppermint, which mice hate, is also a handy trick to avoid an infestation in your kitchen.

The floors of the freezer, kitchen, and storage areas should also be cleaned on a regular basis, as food can accumulate there.

ORDERING FOOD: A METHOD TO THE MADNESS

Ordering is a beast, especially when feeding a large number of people. It is surprisingly complex, so a chef or sous chef will usually be the ones doing this. Orders must be put together while addressing management of food costs, menu design, and cost effectiveness.

When experienced chefs order food, they will go through their desired menu and divide the ingredients into: *a.)* items that are definitely needed, *b.)* items that there is already plenty of, and *c.)* items that they are unsure if they have enough of or not.

For instance, say that we want to make some chili. We know that we have several cans of beans in storage, but we are out of ground beef, so we will make a note to order it.

But knowing that ground beef is needed is not enough. For instance, maybe we want to order more than is needed for this one dish because we plan on making other meals with this ingredient soon. We also want to replenish our supply if ground beef is an ingredient we use often. But, how much should we order for the chili alone?

Generally, the formula for figuring out what amounts to order is below:

How much food should I order?		
(standard serving portion)		
Per person:	2.5 oz.	Starch or Vegetable (side)
	4 oz.	Protein or Entrée Item

However, you should always tweak these amounts slightly depending on your audience. Say that you are catering for a group of vegetarians; you might want to make sure that you have more than the recommended 2.5 ounces of vegetables per person for them, or more than 4 oz. of a steak if you are serving a group of larger men.

When ordering, make sure to specify brand names and "no substitutions" if this is important to you. Many times, if no brand or quality level is specified, the lowest quality or cheapest item will be provided.

It also helps to have strong relationships with your suppliers when ordering. The more your sales representative knows and is invested in your business, the better he can be at his job, and the more you benefit.

I always recommend ordering from smaller local suppliers, as this often means fresher, healthier goods and more individual attention, even if you are a lower-volume customer. (However, in general your supplier will be making more money from their higher-volume clients. Customers who order larger quantities of food will have more bargaining power than customers who only order small amounts.)

Once you establish a steady partnership, ordering from local farmers can be especially beneficial because you can tell him/her what products you would like to see more of and agree to purchase next season. The farmer can them plant accordingly and be able to count upon your business for the resulting produce— a win-win. Many will be happy to do this as they often don't have the luxury of having corporate agreements like larger industrial farms. However, though there are important benefits, this type of arrangement can be more expensive, as they have to invest personally in their equipment and are more vulnerable to environmental factors like drought or crop failure.

Often, small local farmers can also furnish produce grown from heirloom seeds, or seeds that have been used for generations at that specific farm. Varieties that result are often unique and not available in a store. These are also more likely to be free of dangerous chemicals and pesticides, and less likely to be GMO's, or genetetically-modified organisms.

You might need to rely on several different smaller local vendors for your vegetables, fruit, meat, etc., especially if you are committed to buying local.

However, many establishments prefer to supplement their local suppliers with at least one larger commercial provider, which can come through with goods that may not be available locally or on demand.

Food costs fluctuate, and are closely tied to overall economic health and global weather conditions. For instance, higher gas prices lead to higher food costs, due to the increased expense of transportating the product.

The US government also subsidizes production of some food-- such as corn[xii], which is not only used for human and animal consumption but also for making biofuels. This leads to prices for corn staying artificially stable, immune to traditional market conditions.

MANAGING AND REDUCING FOOD WASTE

Today in the United States, approximately 40% of our food goes uneaten and ends up as *food waste*[xiii]. This food not only misses the opportunity to nourish Americans (with approximately 13% of US households in 2015 considered *food insecure,*[xiv] or having irregular access to adequate food), but also contributes to the crisis of global warming by producing methane gas as it decomposes in landfills.

There are many solutions to this large problem. There is *composting,* or controlled decomposition of organic material. Many private citizens and neighborhoods have composting piles, where food waste is decomposed via heat and worms. Quite simply, the food waste is put into a pile outdoors and covered with leaves. The heat of the resulting decomposition will attract worms, which ensure that the waste turns into rich, useable soil. (Composting worms can also be purchased for areas where they do not naturally occur in sufficient numbers.)

Recycling glass, paper, metals, plastics, and other materials can also be utilized so that these do not get thrown away. Most cities will offer recycling plants, with pick-up at private residences and businesses. Many local stores (such as supermarkets or department stores such as Target) will also offer facilities where people can drop off recyclable goods for processing.

And finally, where these services are not provided, there are many companies that have sprung up in recent years that would be happy to pick up your food or material waste. At the very least, you might be able to find a place to drop off refuse.

Items going into the garbage should be a last resort!

As mentioned earlier in the chapter, a lot of food waste can be prevented by knowing how much food to order and being creative with leftovers. Food can also be cryovacced, canned, or frozen if use can safely be anticipated later.

However, there is a component to restaurant culture that makes even the most careful of establishments capable of creating food waste: the fear of running out of food. This is the worst possible situation that a restaurant can find itself in.

Therefore, they would rather err on the side of caution and prepare too much food, rather than risk having too little. Chefs usually direct staff to make more rather than less, and most restaurants (with very few exceptions) will have leftovers at the end of the day. Sometimes, despite all the precautions (using leftovers later, composting, recycling), food waste will be present in some amount.

Supermarkets are especially guilty of wasting food. Since they often cannot sell products past their expiration date, they will simply choose to throw out the food. The film *Just Eat It: A Food Waste Movie* depicts several dumpsters full of slightly expired, but still edible product being tossed out by stores.

Many supermarkets do not donate leftovers, and various shelters and food pantries will not stock even slightly expired food, due to the fear of somehow being sued. This is a shame because there has never been a case of a donor being dragged into litigation for this reason!

In short, there are many tools and means by which you can reduce your organization's food waste. The hardest part might be putting together the dedication and good will to accomplish this.

5. Menu Design & Food Costs

"Do not compromise on the quality and your customers will not negotiate on the price."

--Amit Kalantri

Food costing and menu design are some of the most important tasks that chefs are responsible for. After all, if you cannot be sure that the food you are serving will make enough of a profit, or if your menu is not designed well, your establishment will fail.

Let's look at the example of a food costing sheet for a stuffed chicken dish (see page 96). The goal of a sheet like this is to *a.)* figure out how much a dish costs to make, and *b.)* what will need to be charged to consumers for this dish to make the amount of profit we desire. (Please note that in this case, one dish of stuffed chicken will serve two people.)

First, we need to look at the ingredients required-- in this case, chicken, sage leaf, prosciutto, salt, pepper, shallots, and butter. We would note the amounts needed in the "Amount" column.

For the "Unit Cost" column, we would need to see what our food vendor was charging us for each of these ingredients. In the case of the chicken, the vendor charges $1.20/ ounce. Since two 6 ounce pieces of chicken are needed (12 ounces total), the chicken for this dish will cost us $2.40. This is noted in the "Total" column.

For the sage leaf and shallots, the amount needed to make the dish and the cost per unit for these are very small, so we will use the standard industry measurement for small amounts (0.0625) to calculate our costs.

Food Costing Sheet: Stuffed Chicken

Ingredient	Amount	Unit Cost	Total
Chicken	2 each	$1.20/ ea.	$2.40
Sage leaf (6 ea.)	.0625 each	$1.99/ oz.	$0.13
Prosciutto	2 oz.	$1.20/ oz.	$2.40
Salt & pepper	1/2 teaspoon	1%	$0.09
Shallots	.0625 oz.	$ .17/ oz.	$0.09
Butter	2 oz.	$ .23/ oz.	$0.46
		Total	$5.57
		Portion Cost (1/2 Total)	*$2.78*
		Final Cost	***$8.75***

However, food costs by themselves are not enough to determine what to charge the customer. When working at a restaurant, we also need to figure in *overhead costs* like rent, utilities, equipment purchases and repairs, and staff salaries.

This is why the cost to eat a meal at a TGI Friday's in Rochester, New York will usually be less than the cost of the same meal at the TGI Friday's in Times Square. Times Square has higher real estate, utility, and tax burdens than Rochester, and so they have to calculate that into their food price.

However, let's also say that the overall volume of customers is far higher than in Times Square than in Rochester. You would think that this would even out the prices of the meals, but let's take other factors into consideration: Since the cost of living in general is higher in Manhattan than in Rochester, salaries for staff might have to be slightly higher to compensate.

To address such complex and varied issues, the food service industry has decided on a *standard overhead percentage* of 33.5% (see below table). Of course, this can always be adjusted up or down, depending on the specific needs of your establishment (e.g. if you have less customer traffic or live in an area with high/ low real estate values).

Standard Costing Table

Cost Per Portion	Food Cost (at 33.5%)
$2.25	$6.75
$2.50	$7.50
$2.75	$8.25
$3.00	$9.00
$3.25	$9.75
$3.50	$10.50
$3.75	$11.25
$4.00	$12.00

Using this table, we can figure out that our charge to the customer for this dish should be $8.30 (since the portion cost is slightly over $2.75, we will adjust the price slightly upwards as well). Pricing it this way should cover the food and overhead costs used to produce this specific meal.

WHO IS YOUR AUDIENCE?

Another element that goes into selecting your dishes and pricing your menu items is the kind of customer you expect to be serving. For instance, a cheeseburger at McDonald's is expected to cost much less than a cheeseburger at a high-end sit-down dinner restaurant in a trendy dining district. Much of the price discrepancy is due to the former being viewed as having lower quality ingredients, but a lot can be said about how ambience or reputation can skew prices.

It is often important where an establishment is located and how it is decorated. Prospective diners usually form opinions about the quality of food served after taking a look at the atomosphere of the restaurant. If it is tastefully decorated, with low lighting, polished wood tables and chairs, and well-groomed staff, people will usually expect the food to be of higher quality and hence, higher priced.

Therefore, in order to attract the more well-to-do customers that a restaurant needs to subsist in an expensive or trendy area, they will need to spend more money and time on property upkeep and strive to offer creative, gourmet dishes.

However, an establishment that depends on high volume, such as many fast food and casual dining places, need only provide as much seating as possible and concentrate on speedy service that results in many transactions, but at a lower price point per customer.

Many food service workers complain about the low starting wages in many restaurants. As far as salaries go, many culinary novices have accepted minimum wage or close to that for the opportunity to work for a great chef. Though earnings are low, the resumé impact and learning potential can be high enough to be worth it (more about resumés in the next chapter). In fact, the competition for positions in renowned restaurants can be firece, even though other restaurants in the area may be paying more.

Of course, most restraurants, regardless of the prestige of the name or chef, face the challenge of trying to provide the highest quality food while still being able to pay the bills.

Due to the various cost-cutting measures and industry modifications (such as the rise of "casual fast food" establishments like Panera Bread and Chipotle), many customers now expect restaurant dining for the cheapest possible price as well.

Therefore, an important concept of menu design is this: Who is your *audience?* Who are you going to be cooking for?

For example, if your restaurant is located in an ethnic neighborhood and is catering to that demographic, you will need to build on traditional dishes from that culture in order for your restaurant to succeed. How can you make sure your menu conforms to the wants and desires of your customers? If there are other restaurants in the area that serve the same type of cuisine, how will you make sure yours stands apart? After all, at the end of the day your success will depend on how well you serve your customers.

This is also something to think about when you are a culinary professional trying to decide where to work. What food interests you? What food are you most knowledgeable about? What dishes can you prepare most skillfully?

However, no matter what cuisine you are preparing, the general rule of putting together a well-coordinated menu is that a full meal will consist of an appetizer, an entrée (main dish) and two sides— typically a vegetable and a starch. Dessert can be offered as a part of an official course or as an option.

Also, unless your establishment is known for a specialty menu, you will want to make sure that your menu includes options for those with special dietary needs (entreés, not just a salad!).

Menus take a lot of work to design and cost out, but it is always important to pay attention to customer reaction and adjust accordingly. Make sure to also check out Yelp, Google reviews, and other review sites on the Internet to see what people are saying about your restaurant.

EVALUATING THE MENU

Once your menu is created and your dishes are being served to customers, your work with menu design is not done! Menus may have to be adjusted or redesigned completely due to the seasonable availability of ingredients or price changes from your food vendor.

There is also the need to evaluate your menu periodically. This means doing a "self check" of your dishes' quality to make sure the product being turned out is the dish that was envisioned by the chef.

There are many reasons that the quality or taste of the dish could change over time: Perhaps the tastes of the ingredients have undergone seasonal changes, or your food vendor has switched to an alternate source for the products you purchase from them. Perhaps line cooks have made subtle changes to the process (such as substituting amounts of ingredients or cooking something slightly more or less than called for) or begun to take shortcuts to make their jobs easier. Maybe a piece of kitchen equipment has started to malfunction or needs cleaning, lending a slightly different taste to the end product.

The chef or sous-chef should be spot-checking the quality randomly to ensure consistency (or in some cases, maybe the new changes actually make the dish taste better, necessitating alteration of the original recipe). So what should they be looking for when doing a menu evaluation?

For every dish on the menu, the following should be assessed:

Presentation/ Plating**:** Is the dish arranged in an attractive and appetizing manner? Or it is lazily and sloppily put together?

Temperature**:** Hot food should have a holding temperature of 140°F or higher to ensure safety standards are being met. On the other hand, cold foods should be around 38°.

Texture: Is a sauce too thin or too thick? Are foods fresh, firm, and crisp?

Overall Taste: Is there a balanced, pleasing taste to the dish? Were the correct amounts of salt, sugar, and flavors added? Is it too spicy or too bland?

Some good advice many culinary professionals live by is that the chef should show you how to make a dish once. After that one demonstration, a skilled cook should be able to recreate the dish from remembering the process and by tasting for accuracy. However, do not be discouraged if you cannot do this right away! This ability does come with time and experience.

SOME NOTES ABOUT TIPPING AT RESTAURANTS

Many customers do not realize that tipping is *not* a reward on top of a server's salary, meant as a bonus for exceptional service. Diners can be offended by the obligation to pay an extra cost in additional to the food and taxes that already can make eating out an expensive affair.

However, let's set the record straight: Tipping is essential because it is part of a server's salary. *It is never okay not to tip*, not even when the service is poor. This is because a server's compensation structure is usually dependent on tips to reach the minimum wage per hour that is required by law. Often, a server will make $3-4/ hour, paid from the restaurant's payroll. To make at least minimum wage, and hopefully more than that, the servier will look to tips. (However, if a server still fails to meet minimum wage per hour, the restaurant is required to make it up from its own funds to avoid labor violations.) Also let's remember that the server is also often required to *tip out*, or share a portion of their tips, with bussers and host/esses. When you do not tip, you are also penalizing these employees in addition to your server.

Therefore, if you do not tip your server for your meal at a restaurant, you are in effect saying that you are unwilling to pay your fair share, as a customer, for the restaurant itself to survive and function.

Many do not understand this because, for the most part in consumer culture today, costs for staffing are built into the pricing structure of the product itself. Though many restaurants are deciding to do away with tipping, this structure is still in place at most establishments.

So how much should you tip? Generally, these are the rules:

Very poor service: Speak with a manager about why you are unhappy with the service instead of expressing your displeasure by forgoing a tip.

Service below expectations: 15-19% of the meal cost before taxes, the minimum required.

Standard service: 20%

Exceptional service: 25%+ (A good server, like any employee who goes above and beyond in their positions, deserves to be rewarded for a job well done.)

A note on modern dining habits: When you receive a discount on the meal cost, such as when you dine out using a Groupon, you are still expected to tip on the original amount.

Restaurants will often include a mandatory service charge for large parties. This is because it is much more work for front-of-the-house staff to serve a large party, and since the total check will often be a significant amount, they don't want to leave receiving an adequate tip to chance or the whim of the customers. This is also handy for serving foreign guests, as they often will not understand the American tipping policy.

Though tipping is an obligation, not a legal requirement, people (and certainly restaurant staff!) generally do not think well of a diner who does not tip or who tips poorly. If you cannot afford the tip, you cannot afford the meal!

Another thing to note is that the tip structure often causes tension between the front-of-the-house staff (waitstaff, host/esses, bussers) and back-of-the-house staff (cooks, dishwashers, and even the chef). The cooks and dishwashers, though they are being paid at least minimum wage, will often become resentful seeing the waitstaff walking away with a roll of cash at the end of their shift, when they are reliant on their paychecks alone.

The waitstaff can also come to begrudge the kitchen staff as they only know that customers are pressuring them (with their earnings on the line) to turn out dishes are not ready as quickly as they would like. They might not understand that the back-of-the-house staff are also under severe pressure at busy times, and also are assisting the waitstaff by making sure that the dishes taste as great as possible.

In my opinion, the best thing restaurants can to do is to cross-train staff to perform, or at least understand, the roles of the other restaurant staff.

After all, running a successful restaurant, or business of any type, is always a team effort!

6. Resumés & Cover Letters

"The most important tool you have on a resumé is language."

--Jay Samit

As some of you may have already found, it takes more than experience and know-how to land a job! Applying for a position can be a complicated and intimidating process.

First, you need a quality resumé that highlights your education and experience related to the position that you are applying for.

Next, you will usually need a cover letter to go along with every job you apply to, especially if you apply online.

While those things are essential, don't forget the considerable power of networking! Whenever possible, try to get an "in" for a job with a friend or relative that can vouch for you. This can often make the difference in receiving a job offer over another candidate who has similar qualifications.

Let's take a look at a sample resumé (or C.V.) below:

Timothy Tucker
123 Dudley Street
Dorchester, MA 02125
(617)555-6954
Timothy.Tucker@mail.com

CULINARY EXPERIENCE

Culinary Training Director

9/2012- 12/2013

Miami Culinary Institute, Miami, FL

•Implemented and developed the Culinary Training Program at MCI based on program created at the Salvation Army in Louisville, KY.

•Oversaw daily operations of MCI's café, *The Root Cellar*, managing current CTP student work-study.

•Catered for numerous community events including The Miami International Book Fair, The Iron Fork and The Lighthouse Project's Dinner for the Blind.

Executive Chef/Culinary Training Director

01/2005- 10/2010

The Salvation Army, Louisville, KY

•Oversaw the food service production for The Salvation Army's Center of Hope; responsible for the preparation of 400 meals per day for the Center's homeless and low-income clients; developed health conscious menu using primarily donated ingredients.

•Created and developed the Culinary Training Program, an intensive, 10-week vocational cooking class for people living below the poverty line; admitted students learned basic culinary skills with an opportunity to apply for an entry-level job in the hospitality industry after successful completion of the course; additional instruction in self-marketing, resume development, workplace ethics and effective communication.

•Since its inception the CTP has successfully graduated over 100 students, many of whom are currently working in the culinary field.

Corporate Executive Chef

05/2001- 12/2002

Culinary Standards Frozen Foods, Louisville, KY

•Oversaw research and development of meals and recipes.

•Reverse product engineering and product development of soups, chilies, entrees and sides.

•Inventory management, including ordering new products and maintaining stock supplies.

PM Line Cook

05/1998- 10/2000

The Mansion on Turtle Creek, Dallas, TX, under Chef Dean Fearing

•Bar: included work with oysters on the half shell, shrimp plates, bars, finishing stocks and soups, as well as cleaning coolers, putting away the meats, icing down the line and helping other line cooks.

•Pantry: included work with salads, hot appetizers, fruit plates, and working with cold items such as beluga caviar and house cured salmon.

•Vegetable: included making all vegetables for the line, frying duties on the line and regular menu appetizers, vegetable entree, first course of the weekly tasting menu.

•Grill: included work with fish and meats.

•Fish: included making as many as twenty sauces a day in a 2-3 hour period and preparing entrées.

EDUCATION

*Associate Degree in Culinary Arts*1998

Sullivan University, Louisville, Kentucky

•Studies included: French technique; American/International cuisine; nutrition; garde manger; butchery, baking and pastry; service and customer relations; business law; hospitality management.

ACHIEVEMENTS AND DEVELOPMENTS

•TV/Radio Appearances: CNN, KET Kentucky Life, KET Louisville Life, Secrets of Louisville Chefs, FOX, NBC, ABC, WFBK Louisville Public Radio

•Featured in articles in USA Today, ABC online, National Culinary Review, L.E.O. Magazine, Louisville Magazine, Snail Magazine (Slow Foods USA)

•2010 Kitchen Manager of the Year, the Kentucky Restaurant Association

•2008 Distinguished Alumni Award and 2008 Community Service Award for efforts to improve the lives of those less fortunate, Sullivan University

•2004-2006 2nd place at the Phoenix Hill Chili Cook-Off

•3rd place in the Illinois Vocational Industrial Clubs of America (VICA) state cook-off

References are available upon request.

Now let's examine all the dynamic parts of the resumé, that allows it to communicate all the information needed to land an interview with an employer.

The first step is to make sure that your contact information is prominent and accurate. This includes your email address, which should be professional (create a new account if you must).

The next step is to make sure your work history, or professional experience, is current (include months and years of both beginning and end dates) and accurately reflects your accomplishments. "Accomplishments" is important because many people think that all they need to do to describe a position is to state a list of duties they were responsible for.

However, you would be well-served to write "Sourced and managed strong supplier relationships, keeping food costs 20% below budget" rather than "Responsible for managing supplier relationships."

An employer will always want to see what you can bring to the table to improve their business; past successes will interest them and more likely lead to an interview and a better job offer.

Note that under the job description for Executive Chef/ Culinary Trainer at the Salvation Army in Louisville, there is not a description of the program that was created and developed, but an added bullet point about the applicant's success in graduating over 100 students. This way the employer can see a clear path from the person's efforts to meaningful results.

But let's say your position included duties that you cannot really say lead to any impressive accomplishments, such as the first listed position as a line cook at the Mansion on Turtle Creek in Dallas. In that position, the applicant was mostly spending valuable time learning from the chef, instead of creating results on their own.

You will still want to include something that describes your success in that particular position, such as the note under "Fish" that reads "included making as many as twenty sauces a day in a 2-3 hour period." This demonstrates the challenge of the position, and that the applicant found success with it-- able to make many sauces in a short amount of time! This will also interest an employer who desires an employee who has shown they are up to the demands of the job, and who will excel in the role.

Next up is listing your education. This section should include not only your history of schooling (feel free leave out your high school if you have obtained a Bachelor's degree or higher), but any relevant seminars you have attended (e.g. "Attendee, Managing a Culinary Kitchen with Today's Technology, Harvard University, Cambridge, MA, May 2016") or certifications you may hold (e.g. "ServSafe Manager's Certification, 2016.")

The "Achievements and Developments" section I have included is optional and should only be included if you have a list of accomplishments or awards that are relevant to the position you are seeking.

Lastly, end the resume with a note at the bottom reading "References are available upon request" or similar. And be ready to present these references if asked! (Make sure to contact people who you desire to be a reference first to ask their permission.)

COVER LETTERS

You might have heard that resumés should ideally be contained to one or two pages (a longer resumé is permissible if applying to a more senior position). Even with an excellently-worded resume, how can it possibly contain all the things you want to say about your experience and your strengths as a worker?

This is where the cover letter comes in. Think of a cover letter as a narrative explaining why you, personally, are the right fit for the job. It should clarify and expand upon things in your resumé. What are some things you would say in an interview that wouldn't fit on your resumé?

Or perhaps you have a gap in your work history (as there is in the sample resumé, where it shows no work history between December 2002 and January 2005). The cover letter would be used to explain that while the person might not have technically worked during that period of time, that they were traveling in Europe to gain further knowledge of other world cuisines.

You can also use the cover letter to expand more on the specific skills that make you a useful employee, and to demonstrate any familiarity you might have with the company you are applying for.

See the sample cover letter below, wherein the applicant of the sample resumé is applying to be a Banquet Chef at the Ritz-Carlton:

Dear Hiring Manager:

It is with great enthusiasm that I submit my application for the position of Banquet Chef at the Ritz-Carlton location in Boston Common. As an accomplished and passionate culinary professional with over 10 years of upper management experience, I know I would be an asset to the Ritz-Carlton team.

Aside from the qualifications listed on my resumé (attached), I would speak to my lifelong love affair with preparing food of all types, running the gamut from spicy Indian cuisine, to decadent dessert creations, to exactingly- cooked steaks. Beginning in 2002, I even explored Europe for several years with the mission of learning how to cook in diverse cultures all over the continent.

However, I never let myself or my staff forget the importance of more mundance tasks, like making sure the plates and utensils never run out, vendors are paid on time, and the kitchen is squeaky clean. I take pride in ensuring that every single dish I send out, whether the first or the last of the night, is cooked and plated to perfection.

Last but not least, it excites me to think of serving the discriminating patrons of The Ritz-Carlton brand. The name itself speaks of world-class, second-to-none culinary excellence, and I would love to lend my talents to its decorated history by unveiling creative and invigorating new fusion dishes, as well as providing savory basics.

Thank you for your consideration, and please feel free to contact me anytime to further discuss my qualifications. I look forward to hearing from you!

Sincerely, Timothy Tucker

This cover letter accomplishes several things: elegantly explains a gap in work history, establishes a personal interest in the job (therefore, the employer can be assured that motivation will not be a problem), and reiterates relevant cooking experience in more relatable, colorful terms. It also demonstrates a familiarity with and respect for the company.

Now, before your resumé and cover letter are ready to be sent off to apply for a job, be sure to look it over carefully once again. Make sure there are no grammatical mistakes or spelling errors (consult a knowledgeable friend or job center if needed). Make any edits that would improve your documents.

Lastly, you may be applying to several positions at a time. However, be careful to never let your cover letter feel like a form letter that you are just cut-and-pasting and blasting out to every open job out there. Be sure to include at least one personalized detail to show why you are interested in that specific job, and at least one problem that you will be able to solve for the company. (Perhaps speak to something you read in the job ad, or something you saw on their website or social media page. The rest of the cover letter can be pretty standard for all positions.)

Then, sit back and practice your interviewing skills!

ONLINE APPLICATIONS

More and more these days, companies are requiring applicants to submit an application online through their website or other electronic means. This can be intimidating and time-consuming, especially if you unfamiliar with computers and the Internet.

The first thing to make sure of is that you have an electronic copy of your resumé and cover letter. Ideally, this means having both of these saved as Microsoft Word documents (usually having a .doc file extension name). Saving them as PDF's (.pdf) is also a good idea, although this type of file is less popular than Microsoft Word files. (Also note that in most cases, a pdf file cannot be edited, whereas a Word file can be.) You will want to have these files stored on a flash drive if you need to apply from a computer in a public place.

Next, be sure to have a professional email address that you check frequently, as more and more recruiters these days will contact an applicant via email initially, and you don't want to miss out on job offers. Of course, make sure to check your email regularly!

The next step is to get online. If you don't have a computer equipped with Internet at home or at a friends' house, many libraries and community centers offer these for use of the public. (Just remember to sign out of all your accounts on a public computer and take your flash drive with you before leaving.)

Once online, if you are searching for a job, check out sites such as Monster.com, Indeed.com, Craigslist.com, and Careerbuilder.com, as well as some local sites such as BostonChef.com. (If you have a smartphone, many of these sites will even have handy apps that you can download.) Consider signing up for an account with one or more of these sites, as you will then be able to upload your resume, allowing jobs in need of employees to search for you and contact you if they are interested.

However, if you want to apply to work for a specific company or restaurant, either go to their site directly or search for it using a search engine like Google.com (such as using Google to search for "Legal Seafoods" to find their website).

The website should offer a section called "Employment," "Careers," "Work Here," "Jobs," or similar, where you can see what positions are open and follow the instructions to apply.

One of the most frustrating things about applying for a job online is being asked to upload your resumé and cover letter, then being asked to fill in the exact same information as on your resumé. This can be extremely frustrating and time-consuming, but remember that Human Resource offices usually conclude that if someone is too lazy to fill out the entirety of the online application/ form, they probably do not want the job badly and if hired, would be a lazy worker who would try to take shortcuts.

Online job applications can run the gamut from extremely short and user-friendly, to long, unnecessarily detailed and repetitious forms. However, once you fill out a few of these, you will usually get the hang of how they work.

As always, be willing to ask a friend or job center if you need extra help.

INTERVIEWING SKILLS

Much of mastering the interview process will actually take place before the interview itself even happens. This means that to make the best possible impression, be sure to prepare for it in advance as thoroughly as you can!

First, make sure you review your resumé to avoid being contradictory or confusing when discussing past positions. Conducting mock interviews with friends or a mentor can also help to boost your confidence and prepare you for the real thing.

Try putting yourself in the position of the interviewer. What would make you want to hire someone? What would you want to hear if you were seeking to fill this position?

You also will want to have your *elevator speech*, or brief explanation of what makes you the best person for the job and what value you can bring to a workplace. Obviously, you may not be reciting this speech verbatim, but it helps to keep it in mind to respond to questions in ways that seems polished and confident, yet genuine and passionate.

Here is an example: "I recently graduated from a very demanding ten-week culinary arts program and am really eager to start using my skills as a line cook. I was the best in my class at knife skills, never missed a day, and really enjoy cooking all types of world cuisine!"

Now that you have your selling points down, you will need to do some research on what makes the place you apply to special as well. This research could be as simple as checking out the company's Facebook page or website. Companies will always be impressed that you took the time to learn a little about them. This information also will help you to write a better cover letter; make sure to refresh your knowledge before any interview.

For instance, saying, "I know that your restaurant just added red snapper to the menu; I loved seeing that as it's one of my favorite dishes, and I thought adding fennel was a very creative touch" will sound much better than a version of "I always wanted to work at a Cape Verdean restaurant… You make cachupa here, right?" After all, they will be interested in what you can offer them, not necessarily what your personal dream job is.

Always remember to highlight the value you can bring to the workplace, not just how the workplace fits your demands as an employee. Be aware that the interviewer will be looking for signs that you would or would not be a good fit for the role you are applying for. "Fit" can comprise anything about you—your appearance, professionalism, manner of speaking, and courtesy in addition to your qualifications, educations, and job knowledge!

Before scheduling a face-to-face interview, some companies will want to interview you briefly over the phone first. When interviewing over the phone, make sure to pay as much attention as you would during an onsite interview.

Make sure that you schedule the interview for a time where you can be in a quiet place free of distractions (though some phone interviews will definitely be "on the spot," or when you answer the phone). Have a copy of your resumé on hand for reference. It is also helpful to use the old call center trick of smiling while speaking on the phone. The person on the other end will definitely be able to hear this in your voice, and you will come off as enthusiastic and eager to impress.

For traditional onsite interviews, you might have heard the recommendation that you be 15 minutes early for an interview. This is absolutely correct! Fifteen minutes gives you enough of a "cushion" in case there are unexpected delays—traffic, parking, locating the exact place you will be interviewing, etc. And arriving early lets your interviewer know that you are a person that can appropriately prepare and manage your time. If at all possible, *never be late to your interview.* First impressions count, and this will not present you in a positive light.

Make sure to dress professionally. Remember: If you have to question if an outfit is appropriate to wear to an interview, it is most likely NOT appropriate! However, simple business casual is fine for an entry-level position, and a chef coat is fine for culinary positions.

Once you are there, try to stay calm and call upon your preparation for confidence. It's okay to be a little nervous; interviewers know that job interviews are difficult for candidates, but will be impressed if you manage to stay graceful and confident, no matter what questions they may throw at you.

Speaking of questions, let's look at some of the most common ones that come up during an interview:

•"Tell me about yourself," "Why should we hire you?" or "What are your best qualities as an employee?" Refer to your elevator speech for this one!

•"How would handle customer complaints about your food?" Explain that customer satisfaction is important to you, and so you would offer a replacement dish if requested. Emphasize that you would not take it personally or become irate. Talk about times you have have faced criticism and/or hostility and worked to defuse or resolve the situation.

•"How well do you work under stress?" Tell a brief anecdote about a time you were pressured at work and how you handled it successfully.

•"What is your worst quality as an employee?" Unfortunately, this one comes up a lot. Take care to admit a fault (preferably something that has no direct effect on the job you are applying for), but also list steps you are taking to correct it.

There are also questions that you should ask your interviewer, both to convey your interest in the position and to get a better idea about your role. These include things like:

•"What does a typical day look like for someone in my position?" For instance, if the restaurant has a slow lunchtime but always has large dinner crowds, you will want to know this.

•"How would you describe the work culture here?" This way, you can get an idea if the workplace emphasizes creativity or toeing the line.

•"Do you have any concerns about my qualifications?" This question will allow you to assuage, or at least address, any trepidations the employer might have about your potential weaknesses as a candidate (and all applicants have them!). Listen carefully and try to steer the conversation toward how you can resolve these worries. Empathise with their fears as an employer. After all, they are taking a chance with all their hires just as you are taking a chance with every position you accept! An ideal match will benefit both of you.

When interviewing for a culinary position, especially at a fine dining or upscale establishment, you may be asked to come in to actively work (without pay) onsite for a short period (no more than 2-3 hours). This is called *trailing* or *staging* (pronounced STAH-zhing), and its purpose is to let your interviewers observe your cooking skills in action before they make the decision to hire you.

Though this may seem like a cheap ploy on the part of the restaurant to get free work out of their applicants, many chefs are justifiably uncomfortable hiring a cook without having had the opportunity to see them work. Keep in mind that this is a very important part of the interview process, and the chef will be looking to see if your knife skills and sanitary knowledge are up to par. Efficiency and overall cleanliness are also qualities they will be looking for.

The good news about this type of interview is that you will usually get a hiring decision right after the staging is complete.

Also keep these tips in mind:

- Not all interviewers will bring up salary in an interview, but some might. If you get a question about this, always respond that your salary is negotiable. This will avoid you giving a low amount (which is what they will offer you) or giving an amount that is too high, leading to them looking for other candidates. Try to steer the conversation back to your qualifications. The actual negotiation is better left for when you receive a job offer. (However, if you are pressed to give an amount, respond that you would like to receive "at least" an amount, but that your qualifications would ideally raise you to a higher rate).

- As much as you think you might need to get that extra shot of energy, do not bring your coffee or drink to the interview. Some might consider it inappropriate to bring a drink into the space of someone you don't know, and you don't want to have to worry about spills in addition to all the other things you need to think about! However, if they offer you a drink there you can certainly partake.

- Make sure to turn off or silence your cell phone if you bring it. Keeping it out of sight altogether is the best tactic.

- Bring one or two copies of your resumé with you to the interview. That way, you can give your interviewer one if s/he doesn't have it, and you can refer to it throughout.

- Make sure you get across your genuine passion for cooking! Don't be afraid to show enthusiasm and an eagerness to learn.

NEGOTIATING PAY

Of course an acceptable pay rate is integral to finding the right position for you. After all, almost none of us work for the fun of it alone!

Firstly, you need to know the market rate for your position in the area. Check out some websites like glassdoor.com or salary.com, making sure the salaries you pull up are commensurate with your experience and education.

Usually salary negotiations wait until the second onsite/ face-to-face interview, or until an official job offer has been extended.

Once you bring up the salary question, an interviewer will usually ask what you were making at your last job. Unless you have already provided this information on an application, do not furnish this information! After all, it is your personal financial information and it would be inappropriate for you to ask what they paid the last person who had your title!

Instead of answering this question, or if the questions are asked during the interview process, say something like, "I was looking for something in the range of $30-35k." Then be prepared to highlight all the reasons why you are worth the pay you are seeking!

COMMENTS ON THE MODERN-DAY FOOD SERVICE INDUSTRY

Though traditionally looked at either as a low-pay, low-skill choice OR a glamorous but high-stress career path, jobs in the food and restaurant business have been undergoing changes due to the continuing shortage of qualified cooks and foodborne illness scandals that have taken place at chains such as Chipotle.

Restaurants have been forced to begin offering more competitive wages and benefit packages to attract workers. Workers have also been demanding better treatment through unions and publically-visible movements such as Fight for $15 (i.e. a $15/ hour federal miminum wage).

Employers have begun offering paid sick leave where it is not already required (as of the writing of this book, Massachusetts has legal requirements for employers to offer this to *all workers*) and encouraging workers to stay home if they are sick to avoid passing illnesses on to diners. (Tipped positions are also beginning to be phased out in favor of minimum wages for all, to discourage front-of-the-house staff coming to work while ill to avoid missing out on tips.)

Additionally, consumers are becoming more aware of the stresses and challenges of working in the industry and of the benefits of eating unprocessed, locally-sourced and organic foods. Food itself is beginning to be recognized as a tool for not only living well, but for healing.

Hopefully this leads to real change and improvement in an industry where "sick day" has traditionally been a dirty word.

7. Choose a Path!

"The purpose of life is a life of purpose."

--Robert Bryne

Now that you have all the basics down: cooking, interviewing, resumés, and cover letters, you are ready to begin working! But what are your career goals? What kind of culinary professional do you want to become?

There are many paths that a culinary career can take. A chef may work at a restaurant, school, hotel chain, a hospital or other healthcare facility, or as a personal chef or food truck owner.

Let's look at a sample job ad for a Banquet Chef at the Ritz-Carlton Hotel, complete with a summary of duties, requirements for education and experience, and a salary range:

BANQUET CHEF WANTED

Hotel/Office: *The Ritz-Carlton, Boston Common*

Location: *Boston, MA, United States*

Job Category: *Food and Beverage, Culinary*

Brand: *The Ritz-Carlton*

Schedule: *Full-time*

Position Type: *Management*

JOB SUMMARY:*Exhibits culinary talents by performing tasks and leading the banquet food preparation staff, while managing all food-related catering functions. Accountable for coordinating menus, purchasing, scheduling, food preparation and plating for catering events. The individual is responsible for delivering a consistent, high quality product with an appetizing presentation. Works to continually improve guest and employee satisfaction while maintaining the operating budget. Must ensure sanitation and food standards are achieved. Responsible for providing excellent customer service.*

EDUCATION/ EXPERIENCE REQURED

- *High school diploma or GED; 4 years experience in the culinary, food and beverage, or related professional area.*

OR

- *2-year degree from an accredited university in Culinary Arts, Hotel and Restaurant Management, or related major; 2 years experience in the culinary, food and beverage, or related professional area.*

- *Improves service by communicating and assisting individuals to understand guest needs, providing guidance, feedback, and individual coaching when needed.*

- *Manages day-to-day operations, ensuring the quality, standards and meeting the expectations of the customers on a daily basis.*

- *Provides services that are above and beyond for customer satisfaction and retention.*

- *Responds effectively to guest problems and complaints.*

Salary Range

$95,000- $125,000 annually depending on education and experience. The Ritz-Carlton provides a comprehensive benefits package for all full-time employees.

The Ritz-Carlton is an equal opportunity employer committed to hiring a diverse workforce and sustaining an inclusive culture. The Ritz-Carlton does not discriminate on the basis of disability, veteran status or any other basis protected under federal, state or local laws.

This may seem like an overwhelming amount of information, and can be rather intimidating. How could you ever grow to become the kind of candidate the Ritz-Carlton would want, who would be able to fulfill all of the listed duties successfully?

You will need a career plan: one that lays out, step by step, how to accomplish your goals, but also one that is flexible enough to allow for real life.

Now let's look at a sample career path plan to obtain the job of Banquet Chef:

1.) Attend Newbury College (est. $40,000 annually) to obtain a four-year degree in Culinary Arts or Hotel & Hospitality Management. For this step, you will need to learn how to apply to a college and have a plan in place to finance your education. This might include filling out the FAFSA (Free Application for Federal Student Aid) and taking out loans.

2.) While attending college to obtain your degree, get a part-time job as a line cook or prep cook at the Ritz-Carlton or a similar high-end hotel. This will gain you experience in your desired corner of the industry and look great on your resume!

3.) Show off your culinary prowess and be promoted to a supervisor or sous chef! Promotions to higher positions can often happen quickly in a restaurant environment as the turnover rate of staff can be high.

4.) Gather your confidence and apply to the position!

Estimated Time to Completion: 4 years.

OR you can choose a more direct route. This path would require more networking, as you will be forgoing a formal degree. However, this could be a better path for you if you cannot attend college full-time or simply are unable to take on the necessary debt for college.

1.) Take a simple dishwashing job at a mid-level hotel like the Boston Harbor Hotel.

2.) In two months, you are promoted to prep or line cook.

3.) Six months later, your great work leads to a promotion as an AM banquet cook. Meanwhile, the current Banquet Chef at the hotel has responded to your networking attempts and been impressed by your developing skills and enthusiasm. He or she takes you under their wing.

4.) A year later, your Banquet Chef mentor announces that he is leaving for a more prestigious and highly-paid position as Banquet Chef for the Ritz-Carlton.

5.) Your old mentor calls to ask you to join his team at the Ritz-Carlton as a Lead Banquet Cook! You will be working under the Banquet Sous-Chef in your new position.

6.) Several years later, your mentor announces that he will be retiring from his position. He has put in a lifetime of work in the culinary industry and is ready to hang up his hat.

However, he has the perfect replacement in mind—you! Now that you have the necessary experience, you feel confident applying to the position of Banquet Chef at the Ritz-Carlton, and you come with excellent references.

Obviously the latter career path plan involves a lot of "luck and pluck". However, the culinary industry is less reliant than others on formal education, so it definitely possible, although would most likely take more time.

Now we will look at what the best career path plan would be for you. Consider the following:

A.) What is your end goal?
B.) What are the job requirements?
C.) What steps will it take to get there?

Let's also consider the *Maslow hierarchy of needs* (we have altered this slightly for this book). This classic tool of psychology is used to explain what fundamentals people need to have mastered in order to pursue their dreams. For our purposes, think of this chart as it specifically pertains to students who want to succeed in their personal and professional lives.

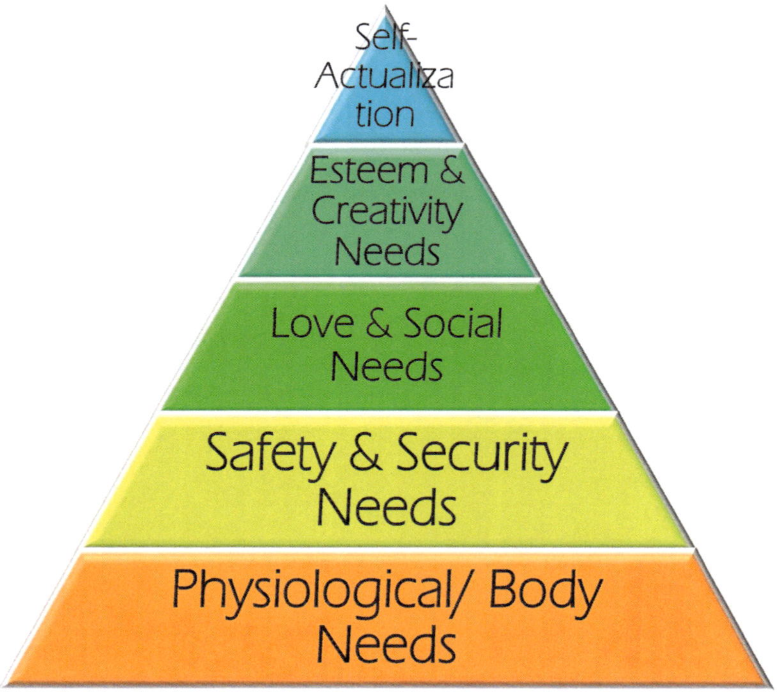

The section at the bottom of the triangle, **"Physiological/ Body Needs,"** describes the most essential, basic needs of any human. Body needs include things like having adequate food, clothing, and shelter. These needs are at the base of the structure because all other aspirations are dependent on these needs being satisfited. After all, without a student's most basic requirements being met, there is no way for them to reach the top section, Self-Actualization.

The second part is **"Safety & Security Needs."** This describes the need to be in a position that is adequately stable and nonviolent and where you feel secure—e.g. a steady home life, where you don't feel threatened. After all, if someone feels constantly endangered and/or feeling vulnerable, they will not be able to wholly focus to achieving their goals.

This is the part of the hierarchy where many people get stuck on "just surviving, rather than living," or where the pure efforts of surviving and keeping one's situation stable and safe exhausts almost all daily energy. For instance, if you are working two or three jobs to make sure rent and bills are paid, that alone might take up all of your time and attention, making you unable to give much effort to things higher up in the hierarchy.

Third, there are **"Love & Social Needs,"** which could refer to a romantic relationship, circle of friends, tight-knit family unit, or religious group that you socialize with. These people or groups will fulfill the human need to be accepted by, interact with, and be supported by others.

Without having fulfilling and supportive social relationships in place, students might find it difficult to gain the confidence needed to reach the next step in the hierarchy.

"Esteem & Creativity Needs" refer to having the self-esteem and self value necessary to be creative. Creativity fills the human longing for self-expression and accomplishment. Pursuing personal creative acts also lead to an increased sense of self-worth.

The highest need is **"Self-Actualization,"** the attainment of higher life goals, building on the mastery of the other needs represented in the hierarchy. Here, the person is happy on the deepest level and feels they are "living the life they were meant to live." For some students, this could mean owning and running their own restaurant or company.

PHILOSOPHICAL GOALS & BELIEFS

For many people, their goals and priorities in the world of work, and in their personal lives, do not revolve totally around money or the dry qualifications listed on many job ads. Their work and efforts must fulfill a deep personal purpose as well.

They may need to see that their daily labors are going towards helping their community, contributing to their religious goals, or helping to further something they believe in on a philosophical level.

If this is important to you, you may want to search out a career specifically at non-profits, non-governmental organizations (NGO's), or religious corporations that align with your values.

However, be aware that oftentimes (though certainly not as a rule!), choosing such a path can lead to a smaller paycheck for the same work. Such businesses are often dependent upon donations, grants, or other non-reliable sources of income and may not be able to pay their workers as competitively as other companies.

Most employees who choose this line of work have often done so for reasons besides money, so it might be worth it to be surrounded by colleagues who share your principles.

TIPS FOR THE WORKING WORLD

Though having a great resumé and killer interview skills can open crucial doors, they won't help you once you accept the position and are actually working. Even if it's in the career you love, your job will not bring happiness and enjoyment every minute of the day. Each position in any establishment brings a unique set of challenges, obstacles, and rewards.

To be a successful worker, you must be willing and able to roll with whatever may occur during your shift. You must learn to deal with stress and adversity with professionalism.

•*Stay professional no matter what the situation*. It's very easy to give into anger and the heat of the moment. As human beings, our emotions dictate a large part of our behavior, and it may feel satisfying to hurl that spoon across the kitchen or stalk out of that meeting, slamming the door after you. It might feel impossible not to tell your boss off during an argument.

However, as a professional, I can promise you that you will regret your actions later. No matter how justified you may feel you are, an outburst at work is never looked upon as good conduct. It may affect how your colleagues and clientele see you, and very well jeopardize any chances for advancement.

A skilled and respectable professional has the ability to de-escalate, not aggravate, a situation. Remember, everyone feels justified when they are angry. When in the heat of fury, they can only see their point of view and how they have been wronged. Challenging them when in this state will only lead to a worse conflict. Allow the person (and yourself!) time and space to cool off. Once the person is calm, they can be reasoned with more easily.

Even if your opinions still clash, professionals know how to compromise and work together to solve problems. (This goes for dealing with coworkers and with customers!)

Of course, we are all guilty of that irritated, terse reply when things are busy, or a short answer to an innocent question when we are attending to other things. These small incidents are understandable, and people usually are sympathetic and will not let it get in the way of a working relationship. However, constructive relationships with our fellow workers and customers are important, and you will be able to accomplish you own aims more efficiently if people view you as easy to work with. Which leads me to:

•*Be positive, even if you don't feel it.* Sometimes you may disagree with your colleagues or boss; for instance, feeling that a certain dish will not succeed or that certain business decisions made by others will have negative consequences. Maybe you feel that you are being paid unfairly or deserve to be promoted when you aren't.

Once again, however justified you are, it is still important to keep a positive, cheerful attitude at work, even if you do not feel it 100%. After all, the situation may be temporary or management might smarten up in a little bit. Try not to let it dim your love of life, or your love of cooking.

After all, positive workers who are able to keep enthusiastic through the ups and downs of business are looked at more flexible, personable, and therefore valuable. (However, this does not apply if workers are being abused or otherwise illegally ill-treated.)

Of course, if you are really unhappy with the situation and have your doubts that things will change, you can always switch jobs (whenever possible, make sure youi have another job lined up before quitting your current one!). But make sure that the same problems aren't likely to turn up in your new position, or you're likely to be just as unhappy somewhere else. And if you change jobs too many times in a short period, you may be labeled as a job-hopper, and therefore a risky hire, for future employers.

•*Never stop learning.* No matter how high you advance in your career, there is always more to learn, more skills to gain, and things you can improve on. If criticism is offered, even from someone junior to you, try to remain humble. They may have a point, and there is no shame in admitting that you don't know it all.

•*Be on time!* This goes for any and every job you have. Make sure to show up on time (though emergencies and traffic jams do happen to us all, occasionally) and ready to work. Being a good manager of your time will make you feel more in control of the rest of your life as well.

•*Be the kind of employee you would want to work with.* Even if you do not personally like them or enjoy their company, getting along with your colleagues and bosses is very important. Recognize that you will not always be working with folks that you easily get along with, but strive to embrace the diversity of the working world and keep good relations with everyone you encounter. After all, there are the people who have the power to either support or sabotage your work, and your career.

•*Don't burn bridges.* Say that you were offered a new position while you are currently working. Think the new offer through carefully and weigh the pro's and con's before deciding to leave your present position. Make sure you give proper notice of your departure to your current job (two weeks is standard in any position) and part on friendly terms. After all, you will be depending on your colleagues for references for most of your working life!

BONUS SECTION: HOW TO REACH YOUR LIFE GOALS
AN INTERVIEW WITH ERIC HALL

One of the most important components that makes the Culinary Arts Training program this book was developed for different from some others is the presence of a Life Coach. Aside from absorbing all the required information about food and cooking, the program emphasizes the importance of students becoming personally ready to achieve their goals and dreams.

Therefore, we present the following interview[xv] with the program's Life Coach, Eric Hall, a longtime supporter of inner-city residents becoming financially literate and successful in the business world. (The interview has been edited for clarity and length.)

Q: Do you think that anyone can achieve what they want (regardless of the circumstances of their life)?

A: Absolutely. As long as they put their mind to it and work hard. It boils down to commitment and if they enjoy what they do.

Q: Tell me about what you feel a Life Coach does, what you feel your role is when you work with the Culinary students, and what it is that you try to accomplish with them.

A: Im glad you asked that. Many people have different ideas of the definition of a Life Coach, but in my opinion, a Life Coach is someone who can help you live the best quality life possible. In order to do that, you must be doing something you enjoy, and you must be fulfilled and comfortable with who you are. You must be comfortable with your past because you need to focus on moving forward. I believe that a good Life Coach helps an individual develop and find that person inside them that they are meant to be-- not necessarily by doing anything for [the students], but by inspiring them to become their best and live their best life.

You are pulling out of the individual what is already within, and getting past some of the stuff that has [been a barrier]. [This means] growing to accept your past, the history of your family, whatever hindrance might be there.

A good life coach can help you to achieve your goals. A life coach does not make a person better, they help [clients] discover who they already are and what they already posess.

Q: Can you talk about any particular student that you saw change in the class [as a result of the Life Skills] or what change looks like with the students?

A: Even as recently as the [Fall 2016] class, I [have had] students talk about how they are applying what they learned in the Life Skills class to their lives. Whether dealing with a family member who is ill, but learning to not let it crush their whole day, or just learning how to move past certain things and believe in themselves, to… take control of their lives and say, I'm responsible for my life. That's when I hear students come in and talk about being able to get that degree, or open a business, or even finish the class. I love when students tell me, "I've been able to make this happen because of what I learned in the life skills piece."

I'm talking about people who have been haunted by past tragedies and are not able to move forward years, sometimes ten or twenty years later. There was a student who never had a job more than a few months. Because of the life skills piece and what he learned in the class, he has now been able to hold a job for two years! These real stories make all the difference. That person just decided that they were going to be better than they used to be.

Even having a winning mindset and attitude about your life can really make the difference in getting the job or contract.

Q: What do you think the biggest obstacle is when it comes to making those changes? Is there a common theme that you see over and over?

A: What holds people up is fear. Fear of the unknown or the unexpected. "I don't know if I can make it through school" or "I don't think I can finish the class" or anything that just seems too big. Fear is a really big obstacle that crosses ethnic and age lines. Whether we control the fear or the fear controls us is what makes all the difference.

Another stumbling block I keep seeing is conformity, being like everyone around them with a kind of "copycat syndrome." Just being on auto-response, or saying "I live my life this way because that's the way everyone else does it," or "I chose to study this subject or take this job because that's what my parents did." What their parents and community are doing might not be the best thing for that student. We are constantly being conditioned by everything and everyone around us, and sometimes it's not beneficial for us. [Students] are often afraid will lose the support of friends or family if they want to do something different.

Q: Do you have any advice for those looking to be a Life Skills coach?

A: Always, always show students the possibilities and their potential. Encourage students to embrace who they are, but still look at areas that they need to work on and develop.

It's also important that the Life Skills coach does not encourage the students to be like him. The Life Skills coach represents only one path to success, and everyone is different. The students should be inspired to take the principles of success: discipline, accountability, and forging your individual path, and apply it to their own lives. They should understand that it all comes down to them.

I'm talking about empowerment: when you are truly empowered in your life, you have all the tools to live the best life possible.

ABOUT THE AUTHORS

Chef Timothy Tucker was born in Springfield, Illinois, and graduated from Sullivan University in Louisville, Kentucky with a degree in Culinary Arts. He began his career working at restaurants such as The Mansion on Turtle Creek in Dallas and The Painted Table in Seattle, but truly found his calling at The Salvation Army Center of Hope homeless shelter in Louisville, where he created a program to teach culinary basics to underserved populations. He established the program in Miami, Florida, and then at the Salvation Army Kroc Center in Boston, Massachusetts. During summers, he is also the chef at Three Mile Island Camp on Lake Winnipesaukee in New Hampshire, and cooks at the Miles of Music musical camp retreat. He resides in Somerville, Massachusetts; you may reach him at Timothy.Tucker@gmail.com.

Amanda Eaton was born in Seoul, South Korea, but was adopted by an American family as an infant and grew up in Rochester, New York. She graduated the State University of New York at Purchase with a Cinema degree and currently attends Harvard University for Public Health studies. She has been a professional writer since high school, when she interned for the *Rochester Democrat & Chronicle* newspaper, followed by a stint as a staff writer for *The Sentinel* in Honeoye Falls, New York. Her writing has appeared in several online websites and journals. She currently works alongside Chef Timothy at the Salvation Army Kroc Center in Boston, and resides in Somerville, Massachusetts.

Endnotes & Sources

Most of the knowledge and training represented in this book comes from the education and career of the authors. However, where specific sources were used and facts cited, the sources are listed below.

---

[i] Parker-Pope, Tara. (2009 March 16). What's Your Cooking Personality? [Web log post]. Retrieved March 18, 2016 from http://well.blogs.nytimes.com/2009/03/16/whats-your-cooking-personality/comment-page-5/?_r=0

[ii] Fleming, Amy. (2013 February). Are you a supertaster? [Web log post]. Retrieved June 14, 2016 from http://w

ww.theguardian.com/lifeandstyle/wordofmouth/2013/feb/12/are-you-a-supertaster

[iii] Welland, Diane. "Taste Perception and Eating Behavior—They're in the Genes." *Today's Dietitian.* January 2008: 38. Print.

[iv] Laird, Eileen. (2013 March 4). Would the Real Olive Oil Please Stand Up? [Web log post]. Retrieved March 20, 2016 from http://www.phoenixhelix.com/2013/03/04/would-the-real-olive-oil-please-stand-up/

[v] Gunnars, Kris. (2015 July). Grass-Fed vs. Grain-Fed Beef—What's the Difference? Retrieved July 5, 2016 from https://authoritynutrition.com/grass-fed-vs-grain-fed-beef/

[vi] Long, Cheryl and Tabitha Alterman. (2007 October/ November). Meet Real Free-Range Eggs. Retrieved July 5, 2016 from http://www.motherearthnews.com/real-food/free-range-eggs-zmaz07onzgoe.aspx

[vii] Guilford, Gwynn. (12 March 2015). 50 Shades of Pink: Here's why your farmed salmon has color added to it. Retrieved September 11, 2016 from http://qz.com/358811/heres-why-your-farmed-salmon-has-color-added-to-it/

[viii] Meyer, Hilary. (n.d.). Fresh vs. Canned vs. Frozen: Which is Better? Retrieved July 5, 2016 from http://www.eatingwell.com/healthy_cooking/healthy_cooking_101_basics_and_tec

hniques/fresh_vs_canned_vs_frozen_which_is_better

[ix] Hardesty, M. (2016 May 7). Personal interview.

[x] Moyer, Melinda Wenner. (2011 July 8). It's Time to End the War on Salt. Retrieved September 1, 2016 from http://www.scientificamerican.com/article/its-time-to-end-the-war-on-salt/

[xi] Bittman, Mark. (2006 November 8). Times Classic: No-Knead Bread. Retrieved July 5, 2016 from http://cooking.nytimes.com/recipes/11376-no-knead-bread

[xii] Urry, Amelia. (2015 April 20). Our crazy farm subsidies, explained. Retrieved September 9, 2016 from http://grist.org/food/our-crazy-farm-subsidies-explained/

[xiii] SDA | OCE | U.S. Food Waste Challenge | FAQ's. Retrieved September 10, 2016, from http://www.usda.gov/oce/foodwaste/faqs.htm

[xiv] Coleman-Jensen, A., Gregory, C., & Rabbitt, M. (2016 September 6). USDA ERS - food security in the U.S.: Key statistics & graphics. Retrieved September 11, 2016, from http://www.ers.usda.gov/topics/food-nutrition-assistance/food-security-in-the-us/key-statistics-graphics.aspx

[xv] Hall, Eric. (2016 October 6). Personal interview.

76865600R00082

Made in the USA
Middletown, DE
15 June 2018